CUCKSERVATIVE

Foreword

The word "cuckservative" triggers conservatives. As a prominent user of the word, I've seen the leading voices in mainstream conservatism react in horror when called a cuck. On Twitter, the very men who complain that society has been too feminized shriek like little girls and block anyone who uses the term. *National Review*, the leading publication of the mainstream conservative movement, has even begun to ban commenters who dare to use it.

What is it that they are afraid of? The word has different meanings to different people. Those who claim to be conservative, yet are unable to answer the question, "what part of America do you wish to conserve?" often claim that "cuckservative" is a racist term.

But for a self-proclaimed conservative to call another conservative racist is hypocritical, and almost serves as a meta-commentary on the term. How often do you hear these same conservatives denounce their opponents on the left as racists? Notice that you will never see the left attacking the left in this manner.

These so-called conservatives are all too willing to attack those who are supposed to be their allies on the right, in order to appease the other side. There is a pattern: whenever a prominent right-wing writer or speaker is attacked by the left, a portion of the nominal right either watches in glee or joins the lynch mob. *National Review* makes a regular habit of purging its leading intellectual lights, including Mark Steyn, John Derbyshire, Ann Coulter, Sam Francis, and Paul Craig Roberts, just to name five, in its ongoing efforts to appease the left.

This book, written by two descendants of the original Americans, will put to rest the lie that "cuckservative" is a race-based term used only by white supremacists. It should also wake up the half-hearted right. The time to please and appease your masters on the left is over. Either join the real right or see us drive you out.

The term "cuckservative" actually comes from the animal kingdom. The cuckold, derived from cuckoo bird, is a man who is tricked by an adulterous wife into raising another man's child, or, as Wikipedia puts it: "In evolutionary biology, the term is also applied to males who are unwittingly investing parental effort in offspring that are not genetically their own." The term has taken on other meanings as well, among which is a strange sexual fetish. That is the larger context illuminating my use of the word "cuckservative".

As an American, I place America and Americans of all colors and re-ligions first. I love my homeland and my people. A Muslim or African-American who loves America and elevates Western values above those of his native land is my brother. Those who reject American values find no friendship with me.

Now, why would I want to see my own people screwed over? I want the best for my people, and I will not rejoice or join in when others seek to use them. And I most certainly will not help outsiders take advantage of my people.

The Republican party, as well as conservative media standard bear-ers such as *National Review* and think tanks like the *Manhattan Institute*, have sold out the American people. Not only do these "conservatives" constantly call for open borders despite their disastrous effects on most Americans, but they have appropriated the terminology of the left in calling all those who oppose open borders "racists" or "xenophobes".

So, cuckservatives are false conservatives who are thrilled to see real Americans get screwed over by immigration!

Open borders are not consistent with Western values. As this book makes clear, a country is not its soil. The dirt is not magic. A nation is its people, and a large immigrant population brings the values of its former homeland—sometimes for better, but often for worse—with it.

Latin America is a mess, and if the people who fled those corrupt and dangerous countries actually assimilated in America, perhaps the "melting pot" theory of American immigration would make sense. Yet as the data shows, Latin American immigrants are not assimilating. Crime rates are higher. Test scores and high school graduation rates are dropping. Latin American immigrants accept lower wages than native-born Americans, driving down wages for everyone, while collecting taxpayer-funded government benefits and consuming expensive public services.

The Muslim world also has its problems. If Muslim immigrants had adopted American values like freedom of religion and freedom of speech, then perhaps a conversation about open borders would be possible. Again, this has not happened. Muslims are more likely to demand accommodation and seek to impose Sharia law on native-born Americans than they are to assimilate and tolerate traditional American values. In some European cities, there are even "no-go areas", designated as such because law enforcement is not allowed to enter the Muslim-run areas without the permission of the local Muslim warlords.

As the two authors of *Cuckservative: How "Conservatives" Betrayed America* observe, there is a thin line between immigration and invasion that is quantitative rather than qualitative. Open borders is national suicide. They should know. They are both Native Americans whose original tribal lands were overrun and taken by immigrants.

of 1965, it has been an article of faith for Democrats and Republicans alike that more immigration, and more diversity, was good for this "Nation of Immigrants". But in 2015, a well-funded American presidential candidate called this 50-year narrative into question for the first time by vowing to deport all 12 million illegal immigrants within two years, shut down the annual $53 billion flow of remittances to Mexico and other Latin American countries, and use the money to fund an impenetrable wall across the length of the southern border. As a result, Donald Trump shot to the top of the polls and shocked the world by becoming the leading candidate for the Republican presidential nomination.

Nor was Trump the only outsider to use immigration as a way to surmount the many challenges posed to those who take on the American political establishment. In the Democratic Party, former First Lady and Secretary of State Hillary Clinton was widely assumed to be the rightful successor to Barack Obama, but U.S. Senator Bernie Sanders, the socialist from Vermont, correctly called into question the false assumption that immigration creates new jobs for native workers and rode that pro-labor position into early leads in the Iowa and New Hampshire polls.

These developments indicate a massive shift in public opinion over the course of the last decade. David Brooks of the *New York Times* observed that there hadn't been much difference between how Democrats and Republicans viewed overall immigration levels during the Bush 43 administration, before lamenting that 84 percent of Republicans and 44 percent of Democrats now believe they are excessive.

What is now taking place in Europe is a microcosm of what is happening, on a larger scope and timescale, in the United States of America. Although the European population of 508 million is larger than the U.S. population of 320 million, the 28 member nations of the E.U. fit into about half the land taken up by the 50 united States. Moreover, unlike the heterogeneous American "nation of immigrants", the European nations are homogeneous and distinct, with long histories, traditions, and collective memories that stretch back for centuries. That is why a much smaller number of immigrants arriving in a much shorter period of time has triggered the powerful nationalistic response that is already overturning governments and will ultimately shatter the European Union.

That is why it is important to realize that the same divisive process is well underway in the United States, albeit at a larger order of magnitude. And one of the tragic ironies of American politics is that it is the very group of people who most proudly proclaim their loyalty to the U.S. Constitution and to the traditional values of America's founding fathers, conservatives, who have helped lead the way to America's decline and eventual collapse. They have done so by forgetting the central purpose of the very document they revere.

The Preamble to the Constitution of the United States of America contains an extremely important phrase that is almost always ignored by those who appeal to it, or to the men who wrote it, in defense of immigration. It states:

> *We the people of the United States, in order to form a more perfect union, establish justice, insure domestic tranquility, provide for the common defense, promote the general welfare, and secure the blessings of liberty to ourselves and our posterity, do ordain and establish this Constitution for the United States of America.*

The key phrase is this: "to ourselves and our posterity." The blessings of liberty are not to be secured to all the nations of the world, to the tired and huddled masses, or to the wretched refuse of the teeming shores of other lands. They are to be secured to our children, and their children, and their children's children.

To sacrifice their interests to the interests of children in other lands is to betray both past and future America. It is to permit an alien posterity, like the newly hatched cuckoo in another bird's nest, to eliminate our own, and in doing so, defeat the purpose of the Constitution. It is, like the cuckolded husband, to raise the children of another man instead of one's own sons and daughters.

It is, in a word, *cuckservative*.

century "melting pot" in the proper perspective, you must first be aware of the three centuries of American history that preceded it.

It is important to remember that the United States of America was founded in a very specific cultural and national context. By the time Great Britain's North American colonies turned to open rebellion in 1775, they already possessed a history stretching back 168 years to the founding of Jamestown. Much of what we think of as American culture was formed during that time. The settlers themselves were overwhelmingly English, with smaller elements of Scots, Irishmen, and mainland Europeans. Of the other Europeans, the largest group were the Germans, who settled in Pennsylvania, and the Spanish who were in Florida and California. And, of course, there were also slaves of African origin among the population, as well as American Indians who were generally regarded by the English colonists as foreigners.

Far from seeing each other as part of some shared 'white' identity, each of the European groups of the time, even those that were closely related, tended to see each other as distinct and separate groups, possessing incompatible and possibly dangerous traditions. Consider the following quote from Benjamin Franklin, written in 1751, when he was still a loyal English subject, as part of his essay *Observations Concerning the Increase of Mankind*:

> *Why should the Palatine Boors be suffered to swarm into our settlements, and by herding together establish their languages and manners to the exclusion of ours? Why should Pennsylvania, founded by the English, become a colony of Aliens, who will shortly be so numerous as to Germanize us instead of our Anglifying them, and will never adopt our language or customs, any more than they can acquire our complexion?*

You may be under the false impression that Franklin's opinion was proven completely wrong by events. After all, his much-feared Germanization of America never happened, and Pennsylvania became a typical English-speaking American place like any other, right? In that case, you would do well to visit Lancaster County and consider the fact that there are now 270,000 Amish living in the United States, more than four times as many as the 60,000 Germans who lived in Pennsylvania at the time Franklin was writing his essay. In 1750, Germans made up about half the total population of the colony, and percentages that large have always had negative consequences for assimilation, even in the long term.

In practice, such numbers proved enough for the emergence of a distinct Pennsylvania Deutsch language, a blend of various regional German dialects. It survived as a primary language for the German-descended population, in preference to English, until the mid-20th century. Even today, estimates for the number of speakers range from 150,000 to 300,000.

So it is clear that Franklin had a point. Yet, you might also ask, is that really a problem? The Amish don't cause anyone any trouble, and on the whole, the German settlers made rural Pennsylvania into a tidy, orderly place. But then, the Germans also made Germany into a tidy, orderly place and a tradition of order is not the same thing as a tradition of liberty. Germany also has a history well known for certain other traditions, which have led to radically different consequences at times during the intervening years. Far from proving Franklin wrong, the history of the German settlers in Pennsylvania shows that the conditions of an immigrant's homeland have more than a little bearing on the habits they can be expected to bring with them to the United States as well as their subsequent behavior as American citizens.

Thirty years after Franklin penned his *Observations*, another writer provided the first known articulation of what we would recognize as the ideas underlying the melting pot. The French nobleman and naturalized American citizen John Hector St. John de Crèvecœur, wrote *Letters from an American Farmer* in 1782:

> ...*whence came all these people? They are a mixture of English, Scotch, Irish, French, Dutch, Germans, and Swedes.... What, then, is the American, this new man? He is either a European or the descendant of a European; hence that strange mixture of blood, which you will find in no other country. I could point out to you a family whose grandfather was an Englishman, whose wife was Dutch, whose son married a French woman, and whose present four sons have now four wives of different nations. He is an American, who, leaving behind him all his ancient prejudices and manners, receives new ones from the new mode of life he has embraced, the new government he obeys, and the new rank he holds.... The Americans were once scattered all over Europe; here they are incorporated into one of the finest systems of population which has ever appeared.*

Sounds like an almost ideal supporting argument for the melting pot, doesn't it? However, consider what made all of that seemingly smooth melting possible. First, an outright majority, at least sixty percent, of colonists were of English origins. Not Europeans, or even British in general, but English, and they were the unquestioned predominant culture nearly everywhere in the colonies. The other settler groups were small and fragmented, with no one group representing more than eight or nine percent of the population outside Pennsylvania. Where English culture prevailed, the Scots, French and others were expected, even pressured, to adopt both it and the English language. Where it didn't, there was no melting that took place at all, but instead the emergence of separate cultures like the Pennsylvania Deutsch. This has relevance to the present day, where a single nation, Mexico, is a source of more than one-third of all immigrants, including illegals, and nearly half of America's newly naturalized citizens.

It is a peculiar, and largely modern, form of wishful thinking to believe that there are no problems to be had from such a large mass bloc of people with a different culture and language. In its present form, it was the product of progressives and social-liberal ideology, intertwined with the blank-slate view of human nature. With the rise of identity politics, the left has gradually abandoned this view in favor of a more open bid for power riding on the backs of unassimilated immigrants, yet cuckservatives still cling to it as a cherished point of faith. Mythology aside, the founders themselves understood the dangers of large unassimilated immigrant populations. Consider the following pair of quotes from two prominent Founding Fathers who are often incorrectly trotted out as advocates of open immigration:

> *The policy or advantage of [immigration] taking place in a body (I mean the settling of them in a body) may be much questioned; for, by so doing, they retain the language, habits, and principles (good or bad) which they bring with them. Whereas by an intermixture with our people, they, or their descendants, get assimilated to our customs, measures, and laws: in a word, soon become one people.*
>
> —George Washington, letter to John Adams, November 15, 1794

> *Although as to other foreigners it is thought better to discourage their settling together in large masses, wherein, as in our German settlements, they preserve for a long time their own languages, habits, and principles of government, and that*

they should distribute themselves sparsely among the natives for quicker amalgamation, yet English emigrants are without this inconvenience.

—Thomas Jefferson, letter to George Flower, 1817

Not only are today's cuckservatives considerably more naïve and pro-immigration than Washington and Jefferson, their views are even more extreme than those of 20th century *proponents* of melting pot mythology. Consider the difference between the following statements by two immigration supporters separated by nearly 100 years:

However great his outward conformity, the immigrant is not Americanized unless his interests and affections have become deeply rooted here. And we properly demand of the immigrant even more than this. He must be brought into complete harmony with our ideals and aspirations and cooperate with us for their attainment.

—Louis D. Brandeis, Justice of the United States Supreme Court, July 4, 1915

When every new wave of immigrants looked up and saw the Statue of Liberty, or knelt down and kissed the shores of freedom just ninety miles from Castro's tyranny, these new Americans surely had many questions. But none doubted that here in America they could build a better life, that in America their children would be more blessed than they.

—Mitt Romney, speech at the Republican National Convention, August 30, 2012

As may be sensed in the collectivist tone of the first quote, Brandeis was a liberal progressive. Yet in modern terms his position on immigration was to the right of the 2012 Republican Presidential candidate's! The Brandeis quote makes acceptance of the immigrant contingent on his conforming to the values of the native population, while Mitt Romney, in complete seriousness, calls someone who hasn't even *begun* the legal process of immigration yet a "new American".

Brandeis's words came at a point in the history of American immigration that was similar to where we are now. The preceding three decades had seen a vast and unprecedented wave of newcomers increase the percentage of foreign-born residents to more than 14 percent of the entire population, sparking serious concerns over the future of the country and its culture on the part of native-born citizens. Notice that Brandeis, writing at the very time the term "melting pot" was coming into popular usage, did not assume that any such melting process would magically take place on its own. The response of his generation of leaders to the crisis was an aggressive program of Americanization, particularly with regards to the education of the children of immigrants, combined with sharp restrictions on new immigration.

Those measures might seem harsh to modern readers, but they were motivated in no small measure by the desire to avoid the fates that have historically been meted out to multicultural societies: either infighting and forcible assimilation to whatever culture eventually emerges victorious, or disintegration and dissolution into separate societies that are held together, if at all, by violence. The measures taken by Brandeis's generation were in many ways successful. They successfully avoided a second civil war, and for decades also managed to avoid the establishment of new ethnic enclaves along the lines of the Pennsylvania Deutsch, much less the Balkans. Notably, and not accidentally, it was during this period that the German-speaking Germans of Pennsylvania were finally absorbed into the broader English-speaking American culture.

By contrast, today's cuckservatives appear to be in a competition with the left to see who can open the borders wider, provide amnesty for more aliens, and add greater incentives for immigrants to retain their own culture in the place of American traditions and values. They do this for a variety of reasons, including self-interested ones, but many of them do seem to genuinely believe in the melting-pot ideal. But is that ideal, and the five assumptions that underpin it, supported by reality?

For example, is it true that the founders of the United States were intentionally trying to create a nation of immigrants? We have already heard from Franklin, Washington and Jefferson. Here is what the leading author of *The Federalist Papers* and founder of the nation's financial system, Alexander Hamilton, had to say on the subject:

> *The opinion advanced is undoubtedly correct, that foreigners will generally be apt to bring with them attachments to the persons they have left behind; to the country of their nativity, and to its particular customs and manners. They will also entertain opinions on government congenial with those under which they have lived; or, if they should be led hither from a preference to ours, how extremely unlikely is it that they will bring with them that temperate love of liberty, so essential to real republicanism?*

—Alexander Hamilton, January 12, 1802

Now leftists could not possibly care less about the intentions of the founders, but cuckservatives do, or at least claim to do so, and appeal to them as an authority whenever possible. And yet, it is clear that the Founders' thoughts on immigration were considerably more dispassionate and realistic than those who believe in the fictional romance of the melting pot.

Did immigrants ever truly come to the United States because they felt some yearning in their souls to become the "New Americans" so meaningfully invoked by Mitt Romney, or as is more likely the case, his speech writers? Does anyone, even anyone who calls for higher levels of immigration, really believe that every individual who comes here does so out of heartfelt love for America and its culture, as opposed to, say, a desire to make money, remit as much of it as possible home, and eventually return there? Fortunately, as it happens, there exists a considerable body of research on this very question.

The first comprehensive Federal report on the longer-term decisions of recent immigrants was prepared in 1908, at the height of the Ellis Island era so romanticized by today's immigration advocates, and the very same year Israel Zangwill's *The Melting Pot* hit the stage. During the very period the modern sepia-toned legend depicts downtrodden arrivals, humbly eager for freedom in their new land, the historical data reveals more than a third of them eventually returned to their homelands. This data provides a crude, but useful tool with which one can estimate the real level of interest of immigrants in becoming American. After all, an immigrant who returned permanently to his home country clearly had no intention of becoming a citizen. The rate of return varied considerably by nationality, as shown in Figure 1.1.

While the breakdown of national origin for immigrants has changed enormously since 1908, the diversity of their intentions concerning permanent residence in the United States has not. A 2014 survey by the immigration research group MATT found that of 600 Mexican immigrants to the U.S. surveyed, only 16 percent intended to remain in the United States permanently, while 68 percent said they intended to return to Mexico. The remainder were undecided. Equally informative were the answers given as to why they came to the United States in the first place. Of the top 11 reasons given, the most common was

on this list had periods of disastrous instability—still, several of them lasted for far longer than the United States has. Intentionally left off this list are governments having the outward form of republics, but without any particular freedom for the inhabitants. The Kingdom of England, not included because it was and is a monarchy, nonetheless for several centuries offered its subjects, in practice, more meaningful freedom at the personal level than most of the above governments.

Besides freedom, most discussions of the uniqueness of the United States, of American exceptionalism, tend to involve a vague sense of the specialness of the place, of America itself. While very few Americans literally see it as a quality of the land, the soil, in the tribal way many in the world see their homelands, they do tend to conflate America, the place, with Americans, the people. The former, geographically, is a lot less subject to change than the people and culture that inhabits it. The unconscious conflation of the two, and the attribution of the relatively eternal nature of the first with the highly changeable second, is most often done by pro-immigration cuckservatives, and underpins any number of assumptions about the ease and permanence of immigrant assimilation. It is of such significance that we have labeled it, "Magic Dirt Theory", and it merits a chapter of its own.

Now we come to what is today a decidedly touchy subject. Are all immigrants in fact equally capable of becoming American? Here we mean American in the comprehensive sense of holding historically American values, as articulated above by Louis Brandeis, rather than the legal procedure of becoming a U.S. person. Since what constitutes American values is both a broad and contentious subject, we'll look at certain specific measures that can be objectively determined.

For example, it is generally understood, even by leftists hostile to it, that American culture has historically placed an unusually high value on self-reliance. One could even argue that the degree of economic

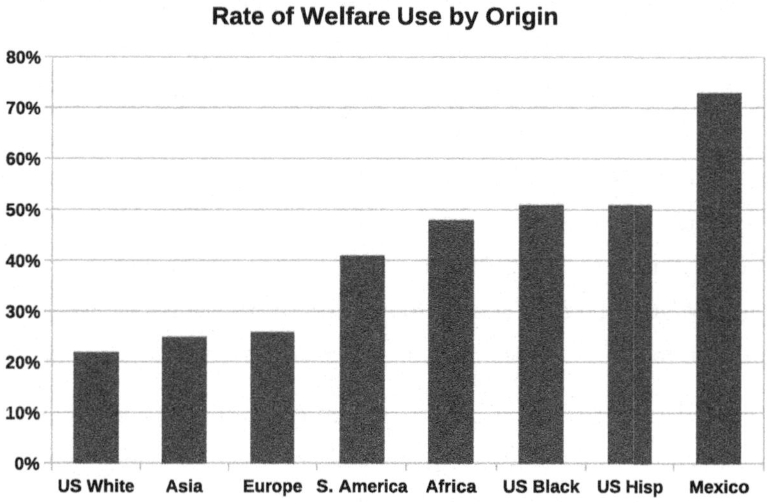

Rate of Welfare Use by Origin

Figure 1.2: Rate of Welfare Use by Origin

self-reliance by an immigrant population is one measure of their compatibility with that value. As it turns out, economic self-reliance varies enormously from one group of immigrants to another.

Figure 1.2 shows rates of welfare use, by head-of-household race or country of origin. Data drawn from U.S. Census Bureau, SIPP (Survey of Income and Program Participation), 2012. The welfare programs counted here include cash, food, housing assistance, and Medicaid:

There is a considerable variance of the rates of return. It is worth noting here that the immigrants with the highest rate of welfare use today also intend to eventually return home at a higher rate than all of the 1908 immigrant groups.

Contrary to a great deal of romantic mythology from today's leftists and cuckservatives, immigrants as a whole, even after twenty years in the country, have a rate of welfare use that is more than half again higher than that of the native-born population.

Another historically American value, closely related to self-reliance and articulated in the United States Constitution itself, is limits on the power of the state. The very idea that there could be constraints on the power of rulers is considerably more rare in history and human experience than Westerners, and particularly Americans, tend to imagine. The forms of limitation defined by the Constitution are very specific to the cultural and legal traditions of England, traceable back to the Magna Carta of 1215, and to some extent further, to the customary limits on royal and noble power in early medieval Anglo-Saxon culture.

The left, in their way, are aware of this. Sweeping aside any limits on the power of the state, or more precisely, sweeping aside any limits on their own power to coerce the individual, whether via government or not, has been the chief goal of the left for as long as it has existed. Along the way, they've sought to change any and all values that supported those limits, by whatever means available, including changing people's minds, and if necessary by changing the actual people. Cuckservatives, on the other hand, tend to naïvely and romantically assume that immigrants, wherever they are from and regardless of the cultures of their homelands, are just freedom-loving Americans in waiting.

But as it turns out, immigrants often hold drastically different views on government from the native-born population. Pew Research Center has conducted several opinion polls, from 2009 to 2012, asking respondents whether they favored a larger government that provided more services or not. Selected results, by demographic, are presented in Figure 1.3.

The extremely high preference for expansive government among Hispanic immigrants is consistent with traditions of government in Latin America since the days of the Spanish Empire. Interestingly, in a 2008 Annenberg Public Policy Center survey, Hispanic immigrants

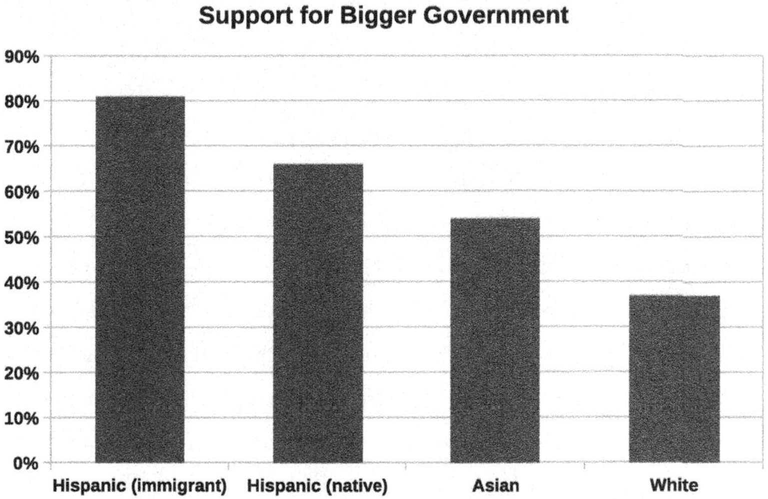

Support for Bigger Government

Figure 1.3: Support for Bigger Government

also supported raising taxes at the lowest rate, 14 percent, of all the identified demographic groups.

Regardless, the fact that Hispanic immigrants are simultaneously the group most opposed to raising taxes, and the group most in favor of expanding government, goes a long way towards explaining the default-ridden financial history of Latin America. If one has the goal of turning the United States into something operating on the Latin American model, importing this attitude would be an effective way to go. There are certainly some politicians in the cuckservative camp who would appear to agree:

> *The Hispanic agenda is the American agenda, it's an aspirational community that I happen to be a part of.*

> —George P. Bush, Land Commissioner of Texas, speech
> in Las Vegas, NV, June 17, 2015

As it happens, George Prescott Bush is the son of former Florida governor Jeb Bush, nephew of former U.S. President George W. Bush, grandson of former president George H.W. Bush, and great-grandson of United States Senator Prescott Bush. Like many of his generation in America's increasingly dynastic political class, he has benefited from his pedigree and the high-level connections that go with it. However, his mother is Columba Garnica Gallo Bush, a first-generation immigrant from Mexico who became a United States citizen in 1979. That he chooses to use his mother's ethnic identity rather than his father's considerably more influential background is revealing of both the current state of American political affairs as well as the trend towards what alt-right commentator Steve Sailer called "the flight from White".

This brings us to the final assumption underpinning the idea of the melting pot: the strength and obvious truth of American institutions. However, it must be noted that those institutions, and their uses and objectives, changed enormously in the last century.

One of the complaints of the generation that revolted against British rule was the practice of soldiers conducting warrant-less searches, whether for contraband or whatever else. Those searches were generally conducted during daytime, and begun with a knock on the door. Today, in many parts of the United States, police can smash in your door in the middle of the night with a battering ram, lob flash-bang hand grenades inside, drag you and your children out of bed or bath at gunpoint, kick or rifle-butt you to the ground if you fail to obey quickly enough, and shoot your dog if it barks too much. All with impunity, without formal charges against you of any kind, and on the basis of an anonymous tip, or merely their own suspicions.

Similarly, the Internal Revenue Service and other government agencies can target private citizens on the basis of their political views, without any consequences for those who ordered it to be done. They can build and train their own paramilitary armed enforcement units, spend public funds lavishly for their personal benefit, and tax, seize, or confiscate property and assets from any number of citizens and classes of citizens, accused of any number of real or imagined sins, and hand them over to other more favored citizens, if they don't simply keep the seized assets for their own use. These overt abuses in the present generation come on the heels of three prior generations of steadily expanding government power, and concurrent decline in the scope of non-political private life.

By whatever combination of cultural decay and demographic changes in the electorate, today's Americans already tolerate impositions greater than those that triggered the Revolution. Leftists, particularly since they made their decisive break with the white working class in the 1970s, enthusiastically support the importation of people for whom the above abuses are not new and unwelcome changes, but the normal experience of government throughout history.

Today's mainstream conservatives, the center-right movement that coalesced after the Second World War, and which has never managed a more positive unifying ideal than William F. Buckley's memorable, if vapid, 'stand athwart history, yelling stop', shares the left's assumptions about the melting pot and the blank-slate view of human nature. They accept most of the moral precepts of the left, and simply want less of them, or for them to happen more slowly.

It is said that a conservative is merely a progressive who is 20 years late. So it is with immigration. Today's conservatives, derisively labeled cuckservatives by their alt-right critics, have been, at best, cowardly and disloyal sell-outs. At worst, they have been active collaborators with the left in the latter's grand project of remaking America by replacing Americans.

Chapter 2

The Magic Dirt

1. "I think of them as a plague of locusts. They go where it's good feeding, bringing their garbage with them. They're rude, self-centered, snobby and only interested in their own well-being." —Sally Janover, Denver, 1994

2. "They are the harbingers of the future. They have compromised their quality of life, and they are looking for other places to go… When people have screwed up their own areas, then they come here." —Gov. Richard Lamm, Denver, 1994

3. "They keep saying things like, 'We did it in California this way, so why don't you change?'… They came here because they liked it the way it was when they visited, but then they want to change it. I don't get it." —Sherrie Watson, Coeur d'Alene, 2007

4. "California has a negative influence on our society. They should keep their world in their world." —Ray Medrano, Las Vegas, 2007

5. "The first thing Montanans hate: Move here and try to turn

Montana into the place you just came from." —Sarah Yovetich, KVGO Radio, Missoula, 2015

These five individuals, from four different states across a span of 21 years, are all talking about transplanted Californians. Despite their differences, they are all observably annoyed with what they see as cultural differences between incoming Californians and the people of their home states, and they're rightly worried that the newcomers will change their cultures for the worse.

Sound familiar? Clearly, all these people must be anti-immigrant racists and bigots, right? But Californians are not immigrants and California is not a race.

If you care to do a bit of further research on your own, you'll find that the opposition to Californians shared by these diverse people, and many others like them, is not aimed at any sort of impoverished and desperate foreigner but at white, American, upper-middle-class individuals. Race isn't a factor and neither is language. Nevertheless, their sentiments are almost identical to the supposedly racist sentiments ascribed to those who oppose mass migration into the United States today.

But are their sentiments valid? Consider whether someone who moves from California, even sharing the same language and broader American culture, immediately drops their old attitudes, abandons whatever life lessons they learned growing up, and entirely adopts those of their new state. Would it even be possible? Even if they did change those elements of their outlook that could be described as Californian culture versus the culture of their adopted states, would that change take place simply because they crossed the state line?

When put that way, the proposition sounds ridiculous. Yet, when discussing immigration to the United States by people from cultures vastly more different than California and Colorado, Americans often pretend this proposition is not only valid, but irrefutable and inevitable. We call this phenomenon Magic Dirt theory, which we define as the idea that beliefs, behaviors, and values somehow appear in particular geographical areas, from the air, from the water, or from the ground, rather than being carried from place to place by groups of people wherever they happen to be.

The concept of Magic Dirt isn't limited to immigration, but is at heart the same irrational and unconscious assumption that lies behind cliched terms like "blighted neighborhoods" or "bad schools". It is the idea that what makes a neighborhood poor and dangerous could be something other than the people living there. It is the assumption that violence, stupidity, and suboptimal life choices happened to well up from the ground in one place, but not another. The same idea is applied writ large to countries, as if some mysterious and unknowable curse causes some nation-states to fail, year after year and generation after generation. It is also the idea that people immigrating to the United States will magically absorb the historical values of America by the simple act of setting foot on American soil.

Relatively few people consciously hold to Magic Dirt theory in such a specific and articulated form. But as an implicit assumption, it underlies a tremendous amount of pro-immigration philosophy. It derives in part from American history and national pride, from the sense of American exceptionalism, from the feeling that our culture and traditions are so powerful, and so obviously right, that others cannot help but adopt them. The belief in Magic Dirt is also derived from the modern conception of the nation-state as an entity defined by its borders rather than the culture or the ethnicity contained by them.

In other words, Magic Dirt theory indicates that the Queen of Denmark is the queen of the land that happens to lie inside the diplomatically-agreed borders of the country called Denmark, rather than the queen of a nation of people called Danes. Americans tend to see these two very different concepts as one and the same idea, when in fact they can be in direct opposition to each other.

Put another way, it is common today to see citizenship in a particular political entity, or even mere residency within its borders, as the same thing as membership in, and identification with, a particular people and their culture. Unfortunately, neither history nor the current state of the world support the assumptions of the efficacy of Magic Dirt.

Is the baby of a Danish tourist or a Saudi graduate student, a child who is a citizen by virtue of being born on U.S. soil, but then returns home with their parents while still an infant, truly an American in any meaningful sense? Is a former Somali militia fighter who arrives as an asylum-seeker in the United States at age 45, and eventually acquires citizenship just as American as someone who lived the same 45 years of their life in Nebraska?

Of course not. The answers to these questions are laughably obvious when stated plainly, despite all the pro-immigration rhetoric to the contrary. Yet, if citizenship doesn't necessarily make someone an American, what does? The answer lies in an understanding of culture. Contrary to the flattering self-image of America, the United States is not even remotely the first country to grapple with the challenge of integrating people of various cultures within its boundaries.

Consider for a moment how nation-states that, until quite recently, possessed homogeneous cultures became that way in the first place. France was not always French, nor was England always English. Both cultures emerged in the Middle Ages, from populations that were once culturally heterogeneous. These changes did not happen by magical effort-free processes, by accident, or without opposition.

Culture, ultimately, is people. Not land, not a region, not an ideological abstraction, but a collection of individuals. People naturally take pride in who they are, in what they are, and for the most part, they want to identify with a group, a tribe they can call their own. They also resist change, often quite violently.

Are all cultures the same? Even today's establishment cultural relativists won't deny differences in fashion, color schemes, music, and the many other superficial trappings of culture. Bring up values, however, and they begin to equivocate. Compare American culture in a negative way with almost any non-Western culture, and our society's dominant leftists will enthusiastically agree, though the occasional cuckservative opposition might raise a few impotent protests. Do the reverse, by pointing out positive traits of American culture versus any other, and leftists will leap furiously to the attack, while the cuckservatives mouth platitudes about how everyone loves freedom and democracy.

As much as it has changed over the years, American culture still has very specific historical roots in English culture and history. Observe that we say *English*, not British, as the latter is more of a multicultural political construct from an amalgamation of four nations than a true national culture of its own. "American" is arguably well on its way to becoming something more akin to "British" rather than "English". Those who value American culture, and who would prefer to avoid seeing that come to pass, would do well to develop an understanding of how America's ancestral English culture came to be.

In the early 5th century AD, the last Roman troops in Britain, facing internal anarchy and mass migration by German tribes on the continent, withdrew forever. At that time there was no English people and no English culture. Instead, the British Isles were a polyglot mix of Romanized Celts, a smaller number of immigrants from other parts of the empire, and various unassimilated Celtic cultures. The Germanic language known as English did not yet exist. The abandonment of Britain opened the way for raids and invasion from Ireland, and on a much larger scale by the continental Germanic tribes of the Angles, Saxons, and Jutes.

It is worth noting that the first German settlers were invited as immigrants, with the promise that they would help defend Britain from other invaders. They were settled on their own land, and even initially given some financial support by local rulers. Needless to say, it didn't work out. The new arrivals grew restless in the small areas given to them, and far greater numbers of their kinsmen began to arrive from the continent. These Germanic tribes fought, migrated and settled, mingling with each other to form a hybrid Anglo-Saxon people who at the same time spread across the entire southeast of Great Britain.

In Britain, as elsewhere in the world, cultural diversity and proximity led to conflict. It was not a war of organized armies, but a struggle of inhabitants who shared the same land, but did not see themselves as the same people. No magic soil maintained the earlier Romano-British culture. It was irretrievably altered by the mass of new arrivals, and was gradually assimilated out of existence, along with the Celtic British themselves, when those new arrivals gained the upper hand. As in many other fields of historical study today, there exists a school of multiculturalists who try to minimize the significance and sheer violence of what happened. Yet the fact remains that the Anglo-Saxons overwhelmed the earlier inhabitants and forcibly assimilated them to their culture and language. As a result, no more than a handful of Celtic words were eventually adopted into English.

The people that emerged from the turbulence held values very different from those of the Romano-British. Late Roman civil society was characterized by complicated hierarchies of patrons and clients with many reciprocal duties, and little in the way of personal freedom. Power flowed from the top down, and loyalty flowed up. This structure sat atop the historically more anarchic values of the Celts. The Anglo-Saxons swept away the Roman hierarchies, and as they absorbed the Celts, a culture of stubborn independence began to develop, with customary limits on the power of rulers found almost nowhere else. It was not liberty to the degree achieved in the countries of Anglo-Saxon descent in the modern age, but the cultural foundations for what would come were laid in this time.

By contrast, the later and more famous arrival of the Normans under William the Conqueror in 1066 was a true military invasion. William, the Duke of Normandy in France, but ultimately of Viking origins, was one of several claimants to the English throne upon the death of the childless Edward the Confessor. He arrived with a fairly small army, and after defeating and killing Harold of England, he replaced most of the local nobles with his own retainers. Because this was a change of aristocracies rather than a wave of mass immigration, the new rulers ultimately assimilated to English culture rather than the reverse. Even so, because the Normans were culturally cohesive, confident and societally dominant, modern English derives nearly a third of its vocabulary from French. The Normans also reintroduced elements of Latin social hierarchy into English society, some of which survive in the remnants of the British class system even today, elements that were rejected by the American revolutionaries.

The important lesson to be learned from this brief historical summary is that nothing about the geography, nothing about the British Isles themselves, or about the preexisting political institutions of the native inhabitants dictated what culture would eventually survive there, or what form it would ultimately take. There was no magic dirt. There was no shining city on a hill. All that was required for irrevocable change was the arrival of sufficient numbers of people with a separate culture of their own who were both willing and able to hold onto it in the face of native opposition.

Nor is England a special case. There was no France and no French in Roman times, and they did not spring up by magic in the centuries since. What we know today as the French language was originally the dialect spoken in the region near Paris, and it became the standard only over the course of hundreds of years of disruption and conflict. In Germany, a similar process produced modern High German. In Turkey, generations of aggressive cultural assimilation, and a considerable amount of large-scale slaughter, by the ruling Turkish minority succeeded in replacing nearly all of the indigenous cultures of Anatolia, long before there was a central government intent on doing so.

Note that superior power, social status, or political authority are not enough by themselves. In Spain and Italy, cultural differences were resolved by establishing long-standing separate political units, and the various regions retained their strong cultural identities into modern times. Nationalist European governments in the 19th and 20th centuries invoked their own forms of the magic soil, and attempted to forge common national identities through ideology and rhetoric. Those efforts have met with mixed success at best, and to this day regional separatist movements enjoy increasingly broad support everywhere from Scotland to Catalonia.

Similarly, successive English governments attempted to anglicize the Irish by governmental fiat, but without mass immigration to Ireland outside of Ulster. They succeeded in spreading the English language, yet Irish culture and national identity remain their own. In fact, the first wave of English nobles sent to subjugate the island in the 12th century eventually adopted Irish culture and formed part of the leadership in various rebellions against the English crown. It is no accident that Ulster, the only region colonized on any scale, is the only part of Ireland still within the United Kingdom.

Much like the Irish, other ethnic minorities that resisted immigration and assimilation have survived many campaigns intended to unite them under geographically-based national identities. Examples include the Basques of Spain, the Flemish and Walloons, mutually, in Belgium, and the Armenians in Anatolia. Meanwhile, both the Jews and Gypsies have managed to maintain cultural identities without even possessing any dirt to call their own, magic or otherwise. And once the Jews did acquire land, they forged a national identity that was based on their own ethno-religious culture, not on geographic or political abstractions.

Or, if all of the above examples from the old world seem too remote, consider the United States' neighbor to the north, Canada. The French colony of Quebec was annexed by the British crown in 1763, after Great Britain's victory in the Seven Years' War. The French-speaking population is in close geographic proximity to the English-speaking Canadians. They originally settled around the same time that the English-speaking population did. Yet they never fully integrated or assimilated, and even went as far as armed rebellion in 1837. In 2015, the Québécois remain a separate people. Less than half of them speak English in an English-majority country. They are kept within the same political fold largely through federal bribery, by enormous wealth transfers from English-speaking taxpayers in the rest of Canada.

All the culturally homogeneous countries of the modern world are homogeneous because their now-dominant population assimilated or exterminated rival cultures within their borders, or because they aggressively resisted efforts at being assimilated into a larger nation and broke off to form nation-states of their own. Both processes were long and arduous, and very often violent. What has not happened, ever, is effortless assimilation, let alone seamless multicultural fusion of immigrants or long-established neighbors by virtue of proximity.

There are relevant examples even closer at hand than Europe. Much of the current debate in the United States centers on immigration from Mexico. Mexico isn't some remote, faraway country, and at many points along the southern U.S. border, there are towns on each side, some no farther apart than the width of a street or two, and separated by no more than a fence. The soil, the climate, the resources are all the same, but the results are not. Consider the following:

> *I had crossed the Berlin Wall several times during the Communist era. I had crossed the border from Iraq to Iran illegally, with Kurdish rebels. I had crossed from Jordan to Israel and from Pakistan to India in the 1970s, and from Greek Cyprus to Turkish Cyprus in the 1980s. In 1983, coming from Damascus, I had walked up to within a few yards of the first Israeli soldier in the demilitarized zone on the Golan Heights. But never in my life had I experienced such a sudden transition as when I crossed from Nogales, Sonora, to Nogales, Arizona.*

—Robert D. Kaplan, *The Atlantic Monthly*, July 1998

The GDP per capita of Arizona in 2011 was $34,676. For the state of Sonora, Mexico the same year, the most recent for which we found comparable data, it was $10,971. Arizona is in the lower half of U.S. states, while Sonora is one of the richer Mexican states. With a population less than half that of Arizona, Sonora has nearly twice as many murders. In the American state, drinkable water and basic sanitation can be taken for granted; in the Mexican state, even in 2015, they can't. In Mexico, paying bribes to police and other public officials is normal, in the United States it is not—though mass immigration and the Obama administration appear to be in the process of changing that.

Did some mysterious force, emanating from the ground on one side of a fence but not on the other, somehow manage to depress the collective performance of one group of people versus another on multiple different metrics of civilization? Or as leftists seem to believe, did the sinister magic of racism, spontaneously generated by the supremacist souls of white people, float across the border to wreak its degenerative evil there? It might make more sense to simply observe that the people on either side of the border have different cultures. Those cultures have different values, and acting on those values has in turn produced drastically different results.

When people holding different cultural values find themselves living in close proximity, in the same neighborhood or in the same political entity, it should be no surprise that to learn that they will tend to disagree on many things. Very often they will disagree on fundamental, and ultimately irreconcilable, things. They will frequently mistrust each other as well, and contrary to at least three generations of liberal-left wishful thinking, talking about their disagreements won't help because the disagreements are material, substantive, and fundamental. The disagreements are not the product of misunderstanding, they are the product of having truly different ideas about how society should function.

From disagreement on the societal fundamentals, conflict, violence, and even war have all too often followed. If, as we noted above, conflict is generated by the societal differences between Californians and mountain-state Westerners, it is supremely naïve to think everything will go smoothly when vast and ever-growing numbers of people from drastically different cultures live in close proximity. The history of past multicultural states is anything but encouraging. A look at the situation in Europe, the behavior of the so-called Syrian refugees, and the rapidly escalating reaction to them by the indigenous European population, ought to cure Americans of their romantic notions of multiculturalism once and for all. Not that it will, but it should.

Even if the juxtaposition of radically different cultures and values within a country doesn't lead to open violence, they will lead to changes in the political structure and the laws. As an example, consider the term 'socialism'. In the American political discourse, the word has such negative, pejorative connotations that even among believing socialists, all but the most fanatical will try to avoid having it applied to them. Even though today's Americans have come to accept a vast array of socialist ideas, from wealth redistribution, old-age pensions, and central banking to Obamacare and the income tax, few still see them that way. Each new expansion of the state has at least met with opposition.

It is very different in cultures where socialism has historically been seen as a virtuous ideal. To some extent, this move to the left is the result of the Melting Pot migration, as the prior wave of mass immigration included significant numbers of people from political and economic cultures well to the left of America's, who left their indelible marks on American politics today. The influence of the left is even heavier in the current wave of immigration, as much of it has come from Mexico, where two of the three major parties are members of the Socialist International.

As a small glimpse of the possible future, Figure 2.1 shows the demographic differences concerning positive opinions about socialism and gun control from the Pew Research Center:

In Mexico, and in much of Latin America, private ownership of firearms is generally illegal, although this has never done much to prevent criminals or cartels from obtaining and using them. As the International Lord of Hate, Larry Correia, has observed, "no matter how many restrictions you put on gun ownership in Nebraska, people in Chicago are still going to get shot."

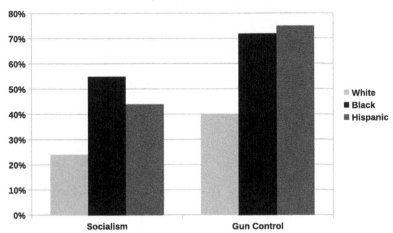

Figure 2.1: Policy Preference by Race

Import people, and you import their culture. Import them on a small scale, as with the Normans, and they may assimilate, but in doing so, they will still influence yours. Import them on a larger scale, and they'll keep their own culture, which will conflict with yours. Import them on a large enough scale, as with the Saxons, and your culture will be the one assimilated. And if that happens, you find yourself at the mercy of whatever the newcomers decide to do with you.

Trust us. We know. Both of our Native American cultures have been all but eliminated. Our tribes were forcibly expelled from their lands and forced onto reservations, where they still live today. Neither of us knows more than a few words of the languages our forefathers used to speak before the arrival of Spanish and English immigrants.

The Magic Dirt won't save you.

Chapter 3

DNA and the Breaking of the Blank Slate

Only a damn fool can expect the people of one tradition to feel at ease when their country is flooded with hordes of foreigners who—whether equal, superior, or inferior biologically—are so antipodal in physical, emotional, and intellectual makeup that harmonious coalescence is virtually impossible. Such an immigration is death to all endurable existence, and pollution and decay to all art and culture. To permit or encourage it is suicide.

—H.P. Lovecraft, September 27, 1926

Racist.

For two generations, few words have had as much power to silence critics in the United States, and to some extent, the rest of the west, as the charge that they are racist. Such has been its power that it came to carry a stigma that could be gained by implication or association, much as the charge of being a communist is often claimed to have carried during the height of the McCarthy era. Those on the left quickly realized the power of the 'R' word, and used it with increasing abandon until by the Obama era, mere disagreement with the president's political agenda was called racist.

And ridiculous as its use became, for a long time it worked. The left was able to use it to variously destroy, silence, or co-opt many of its opponents. Today, cuckservatives still panic and run at the merest hint they might be called racist for taking some particular political position. Yet, in the broader general culture of the west, it is losing that power for several reasons. One is the left's own overuse and indiscriminate application of the term. When the SJW icon and former get-rich-quick marketer Anita Sarkeesian declared, in complete seriousness, that "Everything is sexist, everything is racist, everything is homophobic" it only served to shine an unintentional spotlight on how absurd the use of such charges had become.

Another reason the charge of racism has begun to lose its power is the emergence of new research in the biological sciences, and the slow, widely ignored diffusion of knowledge from that research among the general population. The steadily growing body of evidence from this research will be an uncomfortable subject for some readers. We'll return to it after a short discussion of the roots of both the concept of racism, and its supposed opposite, the blank-slate view of human nature.

Dictionary.com offers the following definitions of racism:

1. *A belief or doctrine that inherent differences among the various human racial groups determine cultural or individual achievement, usually involving the idea that one's own race is superior and has the right to dominate others or that a particular racial group is inferior to the others.*

2. *A policy, system of government, etc., based upon or fostering such a doctrine; discrimination.*

3. *Hatred or intolerance of another race or other races.*

The first definition reveals the agenda on the part of whoever wrote the entry, as it combines two separate ideas that do not, in fact inevitably go together. The latter, the idea that one's own race, however defined, has the right to dominate others is an ideological and political position in line with the second and third definitions, while the former is actually a postulate about the nature of reality, one that can be proven or disproven by facts.

The word racism itself is far more recent than is generally thought. Dictionary.com suggests it originated in French, where it emerged circa 1865. The *Oxford English Dictionary* attributes its first use in English to 1902. However, it did not come into general usage until the 1930s. The concept of race is of course far older, but contrary to modern perception, it historically meant something more akin to ethnicity or tribe and it was common through the end of the 19th century to speak of things such as the "Anglo-Saxon race".

Now why, you might ask, is all this relevant? Because the use of the terms racism and racist, nearly always as an attack, became prominent at the same time as the blank-slate view of human nature. The middle and late 20th century were dominated by the triumph of nurture over nature in diverse fields from psychology to biology. Blank-slate views of human nature hold, to varying degrees of absolutism, that there are no intrinsic differences in aptitude, tendency, or interest among human beings—not only in terms of category, such as ethnic groups or gender, but even as individuals.

The blank-slate idea of human nature was behind Soviet attempts to create a new innately collectivist Soviet Man through brute force of propaganda and indoctrination. To put it mildly, that didn't work out well. The blank-slate view of the human mind is behind every piece of pop-psychological babble that some criminal's actions are society's fault rather than his own. A blank-slate view of biological gender is one of the several mutually incompatible threads that runs through feminist thought, and it is behind the quixotic idea that men and women are naturally identical when not artificially molded into differing roles by society.

In the extreme form taken by some today, the blank-slate idea has led people to absurd, magical thinking, for example that pregnancy and reproduction are social constructs, that a man can become a woman simply by saying he is, or that some people are not humans at all, but *otherkin*, which is to say elves, vampires or dragons, just because they feel like it. So far, the blank-slaters have resisted extending this extremely loose standard to race, but a few brave souls like Rachel Dolezal, Shaun King, and Godfrey Elfwick have recently been trying to find ways around this final barrier through the marginal, but very real concept of "transracialism".

> *I am WrongSkin. You may not have heard of that but it means I was born to white parents and have white skin but I identify as being black. It's not a joke. It's not OK to mock us. It's not easy to live like this.*
>
> —Godfrey Elfwick

So brave.

And yet, not even the most inveterate blank-slatist is a consistent believer in this malleable view of human nature. The snide use of the term "testosterone poisoning" by some feminists and their sympathizers is in fact an assertion of intrinsic biological superiority of women over men. Gay activists found the means they needed to win acceptance when research in the 1980s and 1990s began to suggest the possibility of a biological origin for male homosexuality. Race and gender identity activists, and SJWs in general, are all happy to adopt innate, intrinsic views of their chosen groups when it suits them. Similarly, activists for equality are usually more than eager to assert that they are more educated and innately more intelligent than most people, particularly those inclined to criticize them.

Not even the blank-slate equalists pretend that all humans have the same skin tones or hair and eye colors, or that they are all of the same height. Nor do even they generally deny that those traits can be passed from parent to child, or that similar physical types tend to run in families. While a touchier subject than physical traits, many, perhaps most people, regardless of political outlook, will at least tacitly admit that personality traits, temperament, and intelligence seem to run in families as well.

Now to take a step back. While there is probably an SJW out there who believes mice are just as strong as elephants, amoebas just as intelligent as dolphins, and that only speciesist oppression prevents them all from flying just as well as eagles, even most of the dedicated believers in blank-slate views of human nature will admit that these different species of animals are in fact...different. Similarly, most will recognize that the forms and abilities of each of those species of animals is adapted to the environment where it natively lives and reproduces.

Even within species, both wild and domestic animals carry traits selected either by competitive pressure or by breeders with particular goals in mind. While not generally considered a political subject, readers familiar with animal husbandry, and especially dog breeding, know that different breeds are recognized as having different characteristics, from size to temperament, to average intelligence. So far, so good, perhaps. For all but the craziest of observers, varying, heritable traits among different populations of animals are a real and natural aspect of their existence. Yet, extend this idea to humans, and suddenly you're a racist.

Nevertheless, a growing number of scientists and researchers are daring to openly confront the blank-slatists, heedless of the name-calling they invariably face. Beginning in the mid-20th century as a counter-current among physical scientists uncomfortable with the sweeping, baseless claims of blank-slate social theorists, it has survived years of concerted ideological attacks, and along the way acquired the informal name Human Biodiversity, or HBD. For a long time HBD proponents operated quietly, either not publishing their work, or keeping to the relative safety of obscure academic journals. Today, despite concerted efforts at censorship by SJWs in the media, findings on human genetics and heritability are widely available online, and discussed in terms accessible to the non-scientist.

The current debate offers a dramatic contrast between the blank-slate view of human nature, and science that points to biology, genetics, and heritability having as great an impact on human beings as they do on every other species in the world. Blank-slatism is dominant at the moment, with the benefit of establishment consensus, ideological passion, social pressure, and the power of the state behind it. It is the official position of the respectable elite, regardless of whether they claim to be on the left or the right, and it is enforced by self-appointed activists who are more than happy to destroy lives in the name of the cause. Giving public credence to even the smallest aspect of HBD can expose oneself to ostracism, ridicule, vicious, pitiless attacks by Social Justice Warriors, and being disinvited from cuckservative and limousine liberal cocktail parties.

Eppure si muove, as the Italians say. The Earth moves, whether we admit to it or not. What do the actual facts have to say on the subject? Let us consider a number of readily observable ones.

Do all humans have the same heritable average complexion? This fact at least is not generally controversial, at least thus far, though ideas connected to it have caused a good deal of controversy in the past. The cause is widely understood, and for those retaining some link to reality, it is fairly intuitive. UV radiation from the sun is not equally intense everywhere in the world, thus human populations have come to vary in their complexions, tending toward a locally optimal balance of the amount of UV-resisting melanin needed to minimize skin cancer, versus the lack of it needed to absorb enough UV to produce vitamin D. Yet for all its obvious visibility, and for all its notorious history in discussions of race, skin color is actually one of the least significant heritable differences between human populations.

There are quite a few other minimally controversial and well-documented examples of human variation based on genetic factors rather than culture or environment. Eye color is known to be both genetic and heritable, and it is far from equally distributed across the world. For example, blue eyes are found in as much as 80 percent of the population in central Sweden, 54 percent overall in Poland, 20 percent in France, a little over one percent in Tunisia, and are almost entirely absent in sub-Saharan Africa and East Asia. Light hair emerged in at least two genetically unrelated ways among human populations. The more widespread is the European type, and as is well known, tends to correlate with lighter skin and eyes due to overall lower levels of melanin. Another form of light-colored hair is found among Melanesian populations in the Pacific, as well as Aboriginal Australians, and is not associated with reduced melanin.

Lactose tolerance, the ability to digest milk in adulthood, stems from a heritable genetic mutation more technically known as lactase persistence. There is increasing evidence that dairy farming was first developed in Europe, and indeed lactose tolerance emerged there between 5,000 and 10,000 years ago. It is found today among almost 80 percent of the European and European-descended population, and at moderate percentages among other historical dairy-farming populations, such as the Middle East and northern India. Meanwhile, it is nearly unknown among the Han Chinese.

Populations in the Himalayas, the Andes and the Ethiopian highlands all show genetic, heritable adaptations for living at high altitude. Each set of traits are unrelated to each other, although they confer similar benefits. Of the three, indigenous Himalayan populations show the most powerful adaptations, stemming from the EPAS1 genetic mutation. Tibetans, Sherpas, and other related people carry measurably higher levels of oxygen in their blood, and have larger lung capacity, faster breathing, and higher cerebral blood flow than the general human population. These traits are recognized by geneticists and physical anthropologists as having been subject to intense selective pressure during many generations of life in the harsh conditions of some 13,000 feet above sea level. Unfortunately for mountain climbers and equalitarians, one cannot acquire them by declaring oneself Trans-Himalayan.

Sickle-cell trait, the heritable genetic mutation responsible for sickle-cell anemia, is in some ways a reverse adaptation, as it correlates with an increased risk of altitude hypoxia. This was first documented during the Korean War, when a disproportionate number of African-descended conscripts died unexpectedly of splenic infarctions during unpressurized flights over the Rocky Mountains. More happily, sickle-cell trait also provides resistance to malaria. Because of that, it became common in parts of the world where malaria was widespread, particularly equatorial sub-Saharan Africa.

At the other extreme of earth's climates, variants of the genes UCP1, UCP3, and ENPP7 found primarily in populations near the arctic circle help the body more efficiently convert energy reserves, such as stored fat, to heat, and more efficiently metabolize dietary fat. Europeans and American whites have also been found to have statistically significant higher basal metabolic rates—energy burn—during sleep than blacks. All the latter characteristics translate to greater ease at maintaining body temperature in cold environments. As with sickle-cell and many other traits we don't have space here to discuss, these are heritable, genetic traits that helped specific human populations survive in their historical environments.

What they are not is a blank slate.

That human height is heritable is not generally controversial, though the extent of heritability hasn't always been clear because childhood diet and health can also have a substantial impact on adult height. Even so, most will admit that underlying potential height varies between families and across populations in different parts of the world. Here are the average heights of men, age 18–24, from three high-income European countries, taken between 2005 and 2014, compared with two low-income populations, with approximately similar diets, from the same region of central Africa, the Republic of the Congo:

Table 3.1: Average Height of Men

Netherlands	183.8cm
Austria	180.0cm
Italy	176.4cm
Bantu	159.0cm
Mbuti	148.7cm

Only an SJW, or possibly a cuckservative under threat of the 'R' word could possibly claim that human populations are the same worldwide in average frame, musculature, and general build. The modern epidemic of obesity, and the historical tendency of upper classes to be better fed and heavier than lower classes have muddled this, but it was long anecdotally recognized that some peoples were bigger-framed and stronger than others. A wealth of more reliable data now exists today.

African-Americans, who are mostly of West African (80 percent) and European (20 percent) descent, have measurably shorter torsos and longer limbs than American whites, with legs averaging more than two centimeters longer at median height. They also have proportionately narrower hip bones and leaner rib cages. These traits are even more pronounced among East African populations. Northeast Asians, on the other hand, have proportionately longer torsos and shorter limbs than Europeans. Nearly all sub-Saharan African populations have relatively greater muscle mass in their legs and hips than Europeans, while Europeans carry more in their chests and torsos. Both carry more muscle overall, on average, than East Asians. These are traits widespread and visibly obvious enough to be considered stereotypical, yet they have been validated by decades of studies, and they are heritable traits independent of environment.

Rather less visibly, African and African-descended men have bone density ranging from roughly 4.5 percent to 16 percent higher than European-descended men. This difference is genetic, heritable, and independent of environment. Greater bone density translates to stronger skeletal frames at any given size, and is an advantage in any situation where broken and fractured bones are a risk. Conversely, it increases weight and decreases buoyancy at any given body size, which is a material disadvantage when swimming.

There are also qualitative differences in the muscles different populations carry on their frames. Training can affect the balance of what are generally called fast-twitch fibers, useful for bursts of intense activity, versus slow-twitch fibers useful for endurance. Even SJWs and doughy cuckservative pundits grudgingly understand that exercise increases overall muscle strength, though few of them seem inclined to put it into practice. However, here again, decades of research have supported long-standing "racist" stereotypes of heritable, genetic differences. West Africans have higher proportions of fast-twitch muscle fibers, while East Africans have higher proportions of slow-twitch fibers than the human average. Combined with the aforementioned body-frame differences, these traits have led to the overwhelming dominance of Africans in world-class sprints and long-distance races in recent decades.

Much as Africans dominate running sports, northern and eastern Europeans dominate sports that depend heavily on overall size and upper body strength, such as power-lifting and various strong-man competitions. This tends to conform to the historical stereotype of the strong, large-framed North European, but given the extreme sensitivity of the subject, data is sparse even today. Even so, evidence is beginning to indicate—despite racial stereotypes to the contrary—that at comparable levels of fitness, Caucasian men have higher arm and hand grip strength per pound of muscle mass than men of other population groups.

All of the above are averages and tendencies, though some are nearly universal within particular populations, and naturally, there are no shortage of variations and exceptions. Blank-slate ideologues, of both left and right, tend to find the entire subject uncomfortable, and so often discuss them as if the exceptions were the rule. As if a short, skinny Icelander or Estonian disproved the average heights and weights in their countries, or the success of Jamaicans and African-Americans in running were, by a roundabout path, traceable to cultural factors, racism, and a lack of options in other sports.

But then, reality tends to be inconvenient.

Now, do all humans have the same average emotional temperament? Here, we enter the realm of serious controversy. In premodern times, when it was universally recognized that temperamental traits tended to run in families, it was commonly assumed, by analogy, that they also ran in larger populations as well. Stereotypes of north European populations as stolid or grim, and of Mediterranean peoples as more emotionally expressive were held by those Mediterranean peoples themselves in ancient times. The blank-slate view has, for a century, flatly denied such ideas as racist. Yet, genomic research now increasingly supports it. One of the more dramatic examples concerns Monoamine oxidase A, more casually known as "the Warrior Gene".

Monoamine oxidase A, or MAO-A, is an enzyme in humans produced by the eponymous MAOA gene. It is associated with a variety of mood- and temper-regulation features, and is characterized by the number of times its basic sequence repeats. This may be a little technical, but important. That number of repeats ranges from two to five, commonly referred to in the shorthand 2R, 3R, 3.5R, 4R, and 5R. And as it turns out, these repeats are distributed very differently among different human populations.

The 3R variant is popularly called the Warrior Gene, and is associated with a greater tendency toward aggressive behavior in response to various negative situations, and lower overall levels of both fear and depression. It is found among 34 percent of Caucasian men, 56 percent of Maoris, and 59 percent of African-American men. The more extreme 2R variant is associated with markedly higher rates of aggression and of criminal incarceration. It is found among 0.00067 percent of East Asian men, 0.1 percent of Caucasians, and 5.5 percent of African-American men.

Does the frequency of the Warrior Gene in a population affect those who don't have it, or even mean that everyone who has it will behave according to its tendencies? Of course not. One of the authors, John Red Eagle, comes from a family where the 3R variant is common, and for several generations some of his family members have had histories of hot tempers, confrontations, and violent physical fights, while others have never been involved in anything of the kind. As always, one must be careful to never confuse the macro with the micro, or the average with the individual. But when discussing society-wide issues, it is the averages, and not the individuals, that are relevant.

Over the years, much has been made of the higher crime rates in the United States vs Europe. Leftists, naturally, have been inclined to blame it on American cowboy culture as well as the sinful, magically corrupting presence of privately owned firearms. Cuckservatives, for their part, are more inclined to stare uncomfortably at their shoes and mutter things about poverty and the need to get tough on crime. To be fair, the actual data in Figure 3.1 does tell a distinctly uncomfortable tale.

The traditional left-wing explanation for the statistically disproportionate amount of crime committed in the United States by Blacks and Hispanics is a social one, as various causes from racism, poverty, the legacy of slavery, Republicans, ineffective governmental policy, and urban decay have all been proposed at one time or another. However, these higher crime rates happen to be remarkably consistent with those of their co-ethnics in Africa and Latin America. In like manner, the murder rates of the White European nations are considerably closer to the non-Hispanic White rate in the United States than to the aggregate U.S. murder rate to which they are usually compared.

It should be noted that the observations concerning Europe predate the current mass migration of "Syrian refugees". As of late 2015, Germany and Sweden in particular are already experiencing large-scale cultural enrichment in the form of rape and other violent crime. No

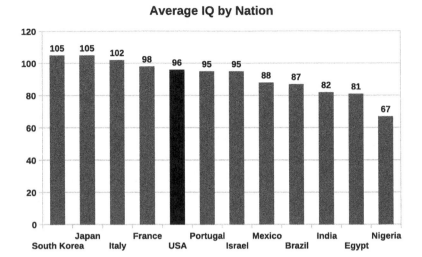

Figure 3.2: Average IQ by Nation

up on a regular basis. But extend that observation from a single couple to genetically related populations, and suddenly you have crossed the boundary into racism.

But reality is what it is, not what we wish it to be. Figure 3.2 shows the average adult IQs from a selection of national populations:

As data of this kind casts increasing doubt on ideas about human equality and other unevidenced assumptions, equalitarian opponents across the political spectrum have usually resorted to one of three defensive counter-arguments. The first defense is that the scientific evidence is lacking. That was occasionally true in the case of 19th-century racialist pseudoscience, but modern statistical research on IQ is methodologically sound and remarkably consistent in its results. The second defense is that the evidence doesn't matter, and the third is that it is immoral to discuss any science or statistics that are related to human intelligence.

Leftists by and large choose the first argument, though they seldom attempt to actually refute the scientific or statistical evidence with any of their own. They usually do little more than attempt to disqualify, discredit, or silence those who provided the evidence. Cuckservatives generally prefer the second argument, and at first glance their position might seem more honest than that of the leftists. After all, if we are all equal before God (or the Social Contract, or the Rights of Man) who are we to consider messy issues like ability, temperament, time preferences, or self-discipline when discussing national policy?

This is not an entirely fallacious argument. An individual with an IQ of 160 and one with an IQ of 75 both possess the same basic rights as human beings. But it is mostly an irrelevant one, as matters of public policy seldom have much to do with basic human rights and any public policy that refuses to take into account the material aspects of human biodiversity is doomed to certain failure.

As for the third argument, the fact that those who put it forth are so philosophically inept that they cannot even identify the moral system under which it would be immoral to observe material human differences suffices to justify it being dismissed as the feeble rhetoric it is.

But regardless of which defense is offered, the history of cuckservative debate on the subject of human biodiversity is hardly distinguishable from that of the left, and it is certainly no more honest.

In the early 1990s, political scientist Charles Murray and Harvard psychology professor Richard Herrnstein collaborated on what would prove to be an epochal project on IQ distribution in America. *The Bell Curve* was released in 1994 to a firestorm of attacks and criticism. Though not the first challenge to the 20th century's blank-slatist ideology, it quickly became the best known by far. It has been reviewed and criticized endlessly in the two decades since its publication, often by critics who have never actually read the book. The bulk of *The Bell*

Curve is a neutral presentation of objectively verifiable data on how IQ correlates to a variety of outcomes in life. Leftists responded exactly as one would imagine, but their tedious, lightweight diatribes are not pertinent here. What is relevant, however, is the response of the conservative establishment to the book.

Herrnstein had died before publication, so the full wrath of the establishment fell on Murray. The cuckservatives initially reacted to the book with uncomprehending shock. A few, perhaps reflexively accustomed to sparring with the liberal-left, even made some half-hearted attempts to defend it. However, once the sheer scale of leftist wrath became apparent, once the accusations of racism began to fly, and Murray's defenders began to come under fire, they broke ranks and ran for cover. To say they threw Murray under the bus would be an understatement. It would be more accurate to say that he was cast into the outer darkness, while mantras to appease the left were chanted.

In the years that followed, *Commentary* magazine began a significant shift to the left on IQ, race, immigration, and science in general. *National Review* followed suit by beginning a new series of purges of editors and contributors who failed to conform to the blank-slate perspective.

The purge of immigration skeptics soon spread to the broader center-right movement. Just as the center-left, during its 1970s takeover by the socially elite New Left, began to attack and purge its older, anti-immigration blue-collar wing, the cuckservatives, who were often of the same social class as the New Leftists (or at least wanted to be), began their own house-cleaning in the 1990s.

However, science proved uncooperative. As more and more scientists conducted genetic research, as the human genome was mapped, and as scientists and interested outsiders began to analyze the data being discovered, the issue refused to go away. The mainstream conservative movement did its best to entirely ignore the new developments. For a brief moment in the early 2000s, it was even possible to see more open and honest discussion of human biodiversity from the center-left than the center-right, although they were hardly happy about it. A prescient article published in 2009 by a pillar of the centrist establishment, *The Economist*, described the quandary as follows:

> *In a nutshell: the new genetics will reveal much less than hoped about how to cure disease, and much more than feared about human evolution and inequality, including genetic differences between classes, ethnicities and races.*

In the years since, the progressive left, of whom the SJWs are the fanatical shock troops, has moved further and further into the anti-scientific realm of equalitarian fantasy, while the cuckservatives of the center right cower in silence. Those on the right who dare discuss the increasingly obvious scientific and statistical realities of human biodiversity are labeled racists, fascists, bigots, and Nazis, often by the "conservative" media. These intellectual rebels have been described by their critics as the alt-right, the neo-reactionaries, and even the Dark Enlightenment, but whatever they are called, they are currently outcasts from the range of respectable, permissible opinion.

But reality cannot be denied forever. The ideological consensus supporting the blank slate is cracking under scientific pressure, and the pressure continues to grow, study by study. However, it must be admitted that with regards to science and human biodiversity, the conservative establishment is for once true to its name; they do seek to conserve an outdated equalitarian worldview that is little more than left-wing fantasy.

Chapter 4

From Conservative to Cuckservative

In the blackest moment of a dying world. What have you become? Look inside and see what you're becoming.

—Disturbed, *The Vengeful One*

Imagine, if you will, a longstanding yet deeply dysfunctional marriage.

The wife is aggressive, domineering, and deeply psychotic. Although not particularly well-informed, or even intelligent, she has always covered for her shortcomings with pretensions of intellectualism, backed by boundless and self-righteous certainty. In like manner, she was never beautiful, but compensated with dramatic clothing styles, unusual hair colors, and an attractive, flirty demeanor. She put the total package to use for many years, attracting a long string of lovers before she finally settled down. Her preferred men were alpha, charismatic, violent, and foreign, but to her eternal surprise, none of them proved willing to commit to her. She eventually married her milquetoast husband due to a combination of happenstance, financial need, and his ready willingness to overlook her many indiscretions.

Years of self-indulgence and living recklessly have taken their toll, and the attractiveness she once possessed is fading fast. She's learned the strutting gangsters and revolutionaries don't pay attention to her anymore, and have moved on to other, fresher prey. The only devotee she's attracted in recent years is an effete, thin-skinned politician who, though an eloquent speaker while in front of a teleprompter, can only pass for alpha if no other men are nearby. So now she consoles herself with radical feminism, exotic identity politics, and paranoid, sadistic cruelty toward anyone within reach, particularly her ever-loyal husband.

The husband himself is docile, appeasing and submissive. Moderately erudite, he spent years silently composing dry, earnest, faintly-spoken critiques of his wife's abusive behavior and suboptimal life choices that he never delivers, but in recent years he has been reduced to little more than impotent grumbling under his breath. He long ago gave up expecting his opinion to be taken into account, and went along with whatever his wife did, although by dragging his feet and feigning incompetence, he occasionally managed to mitigate the damage she caused. In truth, he lives in terror of his wife's disapproval, and will turn with indignant fury on anyone who dares to openly challenge her or the assumptions on which they have built their mutually unhappy life together.

Though his wife was never interested in him sexually, and in fact mocked his inadequacies at every opportunity, she's borne him two children during their marriage. Neither of them look anything like him. In addition to her biological children, they've adopted three more, all from impoverished, violent countries, all three of whom are older than their actual children. All five of them still live at home; the adopted children have had various difficulties adapting to life in their suburban neighborhood.

Despite their marital troubles, the couple has been fairly successful financially. Between his white collar job, her well-connected friends, lawsuits and lavish government benefits, they've become fairly wealthy. Despite the challenges, after all these years, he's gotten... comfortable. He wants to be respectable, and the kids—he tries to think of them as his—might not rob the neighbors again this year. Meanwhile, she alternates violently between declaring that she doesn't need any man and trying to convince her husband to let her most recent lover move in with them. Her husband does his best to pretend not to hear her when she's in one of her moods.

The husband worries that, despite his present prosperity, everything is slipping away beneath his feet. Some of the nicer neighbors have died or moved away, and strangers have moved in with attitudes more compatible with his wife's violent brood of children. In his neighborhood, and others in their area, more and more people are falling into financial difficulties and selling their homes, or are finding their businesses shut down by the local governments. A few people, mostly his wife's friends, are buying up those properties cheaply and are getting richer and richer by making them available to low-income, government-funded renters. He prevents himself from thinking too deeply about the situation by attacking anyone who dares mention any of it in his presence. He's secretly affixed a 'father and patriarch' sticker to the inside of the collar she makes him wear. He's terrified she'll find it, but it does make him feel a little better... and that's what counts, isn't it?

This may sound like a ridiculous situation, but this dysfunctional marriage is metaphorically real, as are its consequences.

Who are these people? What kind of person would put up with such an awful spouse, let alone spend decades of miserable codependence with them? On the very small chance you haven't figured it out, the wife is the Left, and the husband is the mainstream conservative movement—or as they are more accurately described, the cuckservatives.

Conservative is a popular self-designation in American politics, if not necessarily an accurate one, and the number of those self-identifying as political conservatives has grown steadily in the decades since its modern adoption as a political label. *Cuckservative*, on the other hand, is a very recent term, first having come into popular use in mid-2015 as an intentionally insulting term used to describe the painfully obvious failures and self-defeating nature of many of today's self-described conservatives. To say it is not a popular self-designation in American politics would be a vast understatement, as there is probably not a single public figure who would be willing to call himself a cuckservative. Nevertheless, it spread with lightning speed across social media because it is devastatingly accurate. And, as Aristotle informs us, the best rhetoric is always based in truth.

The word *cuckservative* is a spliced-together combination, or in linguistic terms, a portmanteau, of *conservative* and *cuckold*. The latter is an archaic term that dates back to at least 1250 AD, and means the husband of an unfaithful wife, usually in reference to him unwittingly raising children who aren't his own. More broadly, it is used to describe a weak and ineffectual man, who either is too foolish to see he's being cheated on or too cowardly to do anything about it. There are similar words of near-identical meaning in many languages around the world, and they are invariably grave insults to which any self-respecting man is bound to take offense.

In modern times, cuckold has also come to refer to a specific sexual fetish in which a man actively derives pleasure from watching his wife in the act of cheating on him, usually while she insults and humiliates him.

The lover is typically much more masculine, alpha, and dominant than the cuckold himself. The left, ever since noticing the rhetorical power of the term, has been eager to repackage it in order to fit their narrative that the right is racist, and have peddled the claim that the sexual fetish refers solely to the combination of a white cuckold, a white wife, and a black lover. This particular left-wing lie can be easily disproven by a short, if stomach-churning, Internet search, but you'll do well to take our word for it instead.

One can't say for certain whether, deep in their squishy souls, today's cuckservatives actually *enjoy* their never-ending surrender to the left, even at a time when the supposedly right-wing Republican Party has majorities at most levels of government. But they certainly act as if they do.

What both American and non-American readers should understand is that however universal the underlying idea may be, the cuckservative is a uniquely American creature. Most of what is considered center-right in Europe would be seen as center-left in the United States, while the various wildly divergent ideologies called far-right in Europe, that range from traditionalist monarchists to national socialists, have little in common with the political spectrum of the United States and virtually no representation in American politics. There are certainly plenty of political figures in Europe who favor cuckservative-style immigration policies for various reasons, and the catastrophic effects of those policies are rapidly unfolding as of this writing, but they're not relevant to this particular chapter on the American political phenomenon.

Contrary to decades of left-wing efforts to equate the American center-right with the European far right, conservatism emerged from, and still pays a certain lip-service to, distinctly Anglo-American cultural values of moderate religious conservatism combined with disparate elements of social and economic libertarianism. In its current form, it is not a very old movement. Its roots are largely in the post-WWII era, and the specific policies it advocates have gradually changed over the years. Just as "liberal" in the United States came to mean something close to the opposite of its classical sense, so too "conservative" now often means something very different than it once did.

In the early 1950s, the dominant political ideology in the United States was center-left liberalism, itself a reaction to the excesses of the socialist, totalitarian, eugenics-loving progressive movement. That to-day's SJWs have re-embraced the progressive label is no accident and would be material enough for an entire book of its own. We have no plans to write such a book, though, since Jonah Goldberg's *Liberal Fascism* provides a reasonable description of both the historical antecedent as well as the modern neoprogressive. With the onset of the Cold War, and the embarrassing revelations of the real conditions of life under socialist rule, the American left found itself going through one of its inevitable crises of confidence.

Into that void stepped a small group of intellectuals who set out to remake the even more shattered and demoralized American right. The older right, though sometimes referred to as paleoconservative by modern writers, actually had no such singular identity at the time. Unlike the United Kingdom, in the United States the word "conservative" had not been regularly applied to any particular political party or tradition. At most, it could be said that the older strains of thought shared a common Anglo-Saxon skepticism of centralized power, and a particularly American suspicion of elites, both foreign and domestic. But none of these intellectual strains were of any serious political influence in mid-20th-century America.

The early new rightists were interested in discerning the deeper roots of historical American political thought, and in turning its various strains into a viable, coherent political tradition. Some of them looked so deeply that they found inspiration from decidedly non-American sources, such as British conservative political thought. The latter was a generally elitist tradition, openly contemptuous of American-style independent citizenry and the freewheeling style of American political discourse. Among the leaders of this Anglophile camp was Russell Kirk, who is generally credited with coining the American use of the term conservative as a distinct political label. His most famous work, *The Conservative Mind*, proved to be quickly and profoundly influential soon after its publication in 1953. Kirk's book synthesized various ideas from diverse 18th- and 19th-century thinkers, most prominently Edmund Burke, into six canons, or principles, of this new conservatism:

1. Belief in a transcendent order, or body, of natural law, which rules society as well as conscience.

2. Affection for the proliferating variety and mystery of human existence, as opposed to the narrowing uniformity, egalitarianism, and utilitarian aims of most radical systems.

3. Conviction that civilized society requires orders and classes, as against the notion of a "classless society."

4. Persuasion that freedom and property are closely linked.

5. Custom, convention, and old prescription are checks both upon man's anarchic impulse and upon the innovator's lust for power.

6. Recognition that change may not be salutory reform: hasty innovation may be a devouring conflagration, rather than a torch of progress. Society must alter, for prudent change is the means of social preservation; but a statesman must take Providence into his calculations.

The astute reader will surely notice that cuckservatism, especially with regards to immigration, directly violates no less than one-third of Kirk's conservative principles, namely, the last two. Cuckservatism fails to respect tradition, as it manifestly does not distrust those who would reconstruct all of society, and it refuses to recognize the possibility that change of the magnitude necessitated by the size of the 50-year mass migration will destroy, rather than improve, the nation.

Whatever the left may say about them, Kirk's principles are hardly the stuff of SS rallies. As a set of ideas, they're not particularly systematic, particularly when compared with more radical philosophies like Marxism and its innumerable offshoots, or at the other extreme, the Objectivism of Ayn Rand. They are arguably more a set of generalized assertions and attitudes rather than principles per se. Even so, they do represent a particular worldview, though it is not the worldview of the Founding Fathers or of the early American political generations. Notice as well that several of these principles are primarily defined by that which they opposed: the dominant left-liberal worldview of the mid-20th century. From their very beginning the principles of conservatism were subordinate and defensive in nature, or less charitably, they were submissive and passive-aggressive in their relation to the left.

Contrary to Kirk's intentions, the purpose of the other early conservatives, and sixty years of ineffectual conservative meandering since, there is absolutely nothing in the six principles that would have inspired or supported the American Revolution. In some ways, in fact, they are closer to the assumptions and attitudes of the very British aristocracy that the American revolutionaries rejected. There is nothing in them that forms a coherent basis for argument against an expansive state, a ruling elite, or even a monarchy and a hereditary aristocracy. There is no mention of citizenship or American national identity, and absolutely nothing would oppose the country's transformation into a multicultural internationalist empire, so long as it happened gradually. All there is, really, is a kind of stodgy reserve.

And so it has proven in practice.

Despite their conceptual shortcomings, the early conservatives were relatively successful. To many, they came as a breath of fresh intellectual air after a generation of monolithic post-New Deal liberal-left dominance. At the same time, their ideas were sufficiently broad generalities that they were fully in accord with the blank-slate, universalist ideals that became popular during the 20th century. They also contrasted strongly with those older elements of the traditional American right that had emphasized the unique importance of liberty and limited government to Anglo-Saxon history. But the broad congeniality of conservatism to the mid-20th-century zeitgeist helped the conservatives reach a wider audience than the purely American base of the pre-WWII right. Because the new conservatives were merely skeptical of the benefits of an expansive state rather than vehemently and passionately hostile to it, they began to build a following from among segments of the American population, such as the post-war immigrants and their children, who came from less stubbornly independent political traditions than the sons and daughters of the American Revolution.

The nascent conservative movement did attract some of the surviving remnants of the old right, including the intellectual forerunners of the libertarian movement, Southern agrarians, and isolationist nationalists of various sorts. Others joined the movement as well, including the dissident Trotskyites and cold-war hawks who later evolved into the neoconservatives. Contrary to what is often believed today, the first wave of conservatives did not include fundamentalist Christians in any numbers. Progressivism developed out of the New England Puritan tradition and many deeply religious Christians supported the New Deal in the 1930s. A generation later, Christians still remained spread widely across the American political spectrum. It was not until the 1970s, when the New Left rose to power and proved willing to openly display its contempt for both Christianity and traditional morality that practicing Christians began their mass movement into the right and the Republican Party.

Needless to say, these various groups did not all get along very well inside the conservative movement, and many of the original conservative theorists—most of whom were unworldly intellectuals rather than organizers or leaders—were in no position to sort things out.

A leader finally appeared in the form of a young, wealthy patrician from Yale. Strongly influenced by Kirk's ideas, William F. Buckley Jr. founded what is to this day the most important conservative magazine, *National Review*, in 1955. It rapidly became a central clubhouse for the intellectuals of the new movement, including Kirk himself. Buckley aimed to make conservatism socially respectable, a thought which had never occurred to any of the first conservatives. To accomplish this in the political milieu of mid-20th-century America, he invited a number of ex-leftists to become senior writers and editors, including the prominent 1930s Trotskyite James Burnham, the longtime Communist Party USA member Frank Meyer, and a former Soviet spy named Whittaker Chambers.

The irony of defending American tradition by turning to those who had once been its sworn enemies did not go unnoticed. For a few years the rapid growth of the conservative movement and of the broader new right overshadowed any infighting, but soon enough, cracks began to appear. In 1957, Whittaker Chambers' review of Ayn Rand's *Atlas Shrugged* triggered a serious and permanent rift between what was beginning to emerge as mainstream conservatism and Rand's own nascent movement. The following year, businessman Robert Welch Jr. founded an organization that combined American nationalism with opposition to foreign military adventures and collectivism in all its forms. This group, the John Birch Society, was named for an American missionary shot by communists in China in 1945. Unlike Rand's Objectivism, its positions were not a comprehensive philosophy, but a set of specific ideas that were generally compatible with the stated positions of conservatism at the time.

However, Buckley and the leadership of *National Review* did not see the new organization as being helpful to the cause. Buckley, as noted, was very concerned about ensuring that conservatism remained socially respectable. The Birchers, as they came to be nicknamed, were less compromising than Buckley's conservatives, and they embraced some eclectic positions, such as opposition to water fluoridation, that made them susceptible to superficial, but effective, mockery by the liberal-left press. Buckley and those around him faced a simple choice between embracing their conservative extremists, or purging them in order to appease conservatism's enemies. It was a choice the left had made many times, almost always in favor of embracing and defending their own extremists.

In what may be seen as the birth of cuckservativism, Buckley and his peers chose appeasement instead, and in 1962 Buckley publicly denounced the John Birch Society and banished it from conservatism. The purge, and resulting schism, formed a pattern that would be repeated time and again in subsequent decades. This choice also signaled something about the emerging character of the conservative movement. Individual leftists have a well-earned reputation for being, to put it mildly, less than brave on average. Yet as a movement, the left's reliably ferocious defense of its extremists, then and now, demonstrates a consistent willingness to fight when it matters. The conservative abandonment of the more extreme, or even merely less moderate, elements of the right signaled the precise opposite. It indicated a cowardly and submissive readiness to surrender when faced with public criticism. And it is a pattern that has held in the five intervening decades.

The following year, 1963, proved to be pivotal in another way. The early growth of the conservative movement had taken place in the shadow of an unchallengeable liberal-left dominance. But in the years immediately after World War II, the mainstream left had undergone a modest, and mostly superficial, move toward the political center. Over the course of the 1950s and early 1960s, this reformed center-left, technocratic and carefully quiet about its true ideology, had proceeded to enjoy renewed success, and even a certain smug confidence, reaching its peak with John F. Kennedy's New Frontier. For ten years, the left had treated the conservatives as an exotic and bemusing sideshow rather than a meaningful threat. But Kennedy's assassination in 1963 shattered the center-left's placid sense of control. Soon the press was filled with hysterical articles addressing the rise of a lunatic 'radical right' that posed a danger not dissimilar to that once posed by a certain Bavarian workers' party to the Weimar Republic. Having already shown they would fold under pressure, the mainstream conservatives went to great pains to prove to all and sundry that whatever they might be, they weren't *those* awful people.

The immediate results of their appeasement and submission were predictable. In 1964, conservative icon Barry Goldwater went down in the most lopsided defeat of a Republican presidential candidate in the postwar era. The Civil Rights Act of 1964, whatever else it entailed, was also an enormous expansion of Federal power in direct opposition to stated conservative principles. And yet, some early cuckservatives abandoned Goldwater during the 1964 election precisely because he had opposed the Act. 1965 saw the passage of the equally expansive Voting Rights Act, and of the less known, yet more significant Hart-Celler Immigration and Nationality Act, which is the subject of its own chapter in this book and is arguably the most self-defeating, self-destructive event in American history, including the Civil War.

Throughout the remainder of the 1960s and 1970s the mainstream conservatives as epitomized by Buckley continued their efforts to achieve respectability by purging extremists. Yet, then and now, the unstated measure of that respectability has been acceptance by liberal-left cultural elites. Naturally, it continued to elude them, as did a repetition of the rapid early growth they'd enjoyed in the late 1950s and early 60s. Having demonstrated an unwillingness to stand up to their enemies, cuckservative leaders faced low morale and dissension among their allies. Many of the various movements that today come under the header of the alternative right originated with those purged from conservatism beginning in the 1960s. The modern libertarian movement, for example, began with intellectuals who were made unwelcome in 1970s conservative circles.

One arguable success of the conservative movement during that era was its association with and acceptance by the Republican Party. For its first century of existence the latter held positions very different from its current platform. It was historically opposed to free trade, skeptical of foreign intervention, anti-state's rights, and to the left of the Democratic Party on most domestic social policies. The only fully consistent trait of the prewar and postwar Republican parties was a general, and often very clubby, pro-business orientation. The conservatives set out to change things. Along the way, they struggled with the older, centrist country-club wing of the Republican Party. The eventual amicable settlement of that struggle marks another dividing point of the right.

Meanwhile, leftists of the same era began to realize that the people, in the form of their old working-class white base, had failed them, so naturally they decided to elect another. From then onward, anti-immigration Democratic politicians associated with blue-collar labor unions began increasingly to lose out to pro-immigrant and even pro-illegal figures who saw where the future could be written. Fear of losing their jobs to imported competitors, along with the sheer open snobbery and condescension of the often elite-educated New Left leaders, began to alienate some of those blue-collar workers themselves. Cuckservatives paid little attention to the demographic aspects of the changes on the left, and tended to assume that whatever was going on, it was about taxes and government spending.

It is largely forgotten today that Ronald Reagan, during his governorship of California, his rise, and his presidency, was far from universally popular with either self-professed conservatives or the established leadership of the Republican Party. It was Reagan who found religious social conservatives, and a fair portion of working-class whites, abandoned in the political wilderness in the mid 1970s, and drew them to his cause. It was Reagan who took up the early conservative call to not merely delay the growth of, but actually reduce the size and power of the Federal government. His success in doing so while in office is open to debate, but merely *saying* that he intended to do so got him labeled… yes, you guessed it… an extremist.

Reagan's extremism nevertheless proved immensely popular, and he almost single-handedly revived the conservative movement, despite the quiet condescension of some of its leaders. The success of his early reforms, and of his foreign policy against the declining Soviets, did much to quiet his internal critics. His re-election in 1984 was in many ways the high water mark of the mainstream conservative movement, and even some who opposed him in that era, such as the neoconservatives of the Bush family, now drape themselves in the nostalgic mantle of his memory. Meanwhile, by the early 1990s, in the immediate aftermath of the 1989 collapse of the Soviet Union, the left found itself caught up in another crisis of confidence. Just as it had during the onset of the

Cold War, the left's mask of messianic certainty slipped to reveal the neurotic, fretful face beneath. As a movement, it was as demoralized and weak as it has been at any time in the past hundred years.

The conservatives found themselves facing an astonishing and unprecedented opportunity to accomplish the many things they'd always said they wanted. Over the years, they'd grown their once-tiny infrastructure of obscure think-tanks and erudite journals into large, well-funded institutions. Now inextricably linked with the Republican Party, they'd achieved broader electoral success than they'd been able to achieve in Reagan's day by taking control of both houses of Congress as well as the majority of state governorships and legislatures. For an entire political cycle, the conservatives and the Republican Party had the power, the real political and cultural power to do more than complain about the left and its policies. It was entirely within their power to stop, and even reverse, the entire left-wing program.

Yet what did they do with it all?

In power, conservatives have acted as if they were still in the shadow of overwhelming center-left control of government, as if nothing had changed in all the years since the mid-20th century. From Buckley in 1963 to Boehner in 2013, they've crawled and compromised and pleaded with the left as if their continued existence depended on it. In truth, all the left could really threaten them with is calling them racist and refusing to say nice things about them in the *New York Times*. Nevertheless, that proved sufficient to keep the brave conservative revolutionaries in line.

For its part, the left's renewed success hasn't come from any inexorable logic of its arguments, which have never stood up well to open debate. From the start, the left has derived its political power by promising the gratification of wishes, the satisfaction of long-standing grudges, and the hope for free goods and services to magical thinkers incapable of connecting cause and effect. When it has had enough power, the left has always been happy to silence its opponents by force. When it hasn't, it has tried to socially co-opt them, cow them, or when intimidation fails, to disqualify them through the use of poisonous rhetoric and ad-hominem attacks.

These tactics have worked all too well on critics who make the mistake of accepting the left's premises at face value. The cuckservatives accepted an inferior, defensive and defeatist role from the beginning of their movement. Many of their founding principles were faint, universalist generalities that have reliably proven to be no defense against the equally universalist, but far more aggressive assertions of the left. In the decades since, they've let themselves be cowed and co-opted into accepting the left's assumption of moral superiority, and ultimately, they have accepted the greater part of the leftist worldview itself. No wonder they've accomplished nothing.

Unless, that is, calling for the same thing as the left, but less of it and twenty years later, counts as something.

The cuckservatives have always been happy to betray their edgier allies and co-belligerents in order to please their enemies. But what is worse is that in recent years, they've become willing to openly sell out even their own base of the taxpaying, law-abiding, and respectable citizens who were drawn to mainstream conservative politics because they were suspicious of an overly powerful state. This is because an embarrassing demographic reality makes the cuckservatives uncomfortable: the conservative base is overwhelmingly native-born and white.

Meanwhile, the left is using the lack of genuine conservative opposition to fundamentally transform the country, culturally and demographically, in their favor. They're doing this at a faster and more furious pace than the most radical leftist dreamed possible. They now denounce opposition to leftist objectives as racist—their favorite and most effective tactic—as the window of opportunity to stop them through the conventional political system rapidly closes.

Yet simply observe as much, and you are immediately labeled an enemy by their so-called opponents. Here's the headline from a July 27, 2015 article on immigration and politics in *Commentary* magazine, by neoconservative John Podhoretz, and it could have come straight from Obama's mouth, or for that matter, Saul Alinsky's: "*Trump: The Case for Despairing—About America.*"

Cuckservatives are not only disloyal to America, they are not even loyal to their own political party. At the time of this writing, Donald Trump has a significant lead in the national polls in the campaign for the Republican presidential nomination, mostly due to his robust position against open borders. And yet, he is being openly attacked by Republican cuckservatives at every level, from governors to political operatives to the token conservative at the *New York Times*, as everything from "a little fascistic" to "a fascist" to "a madman who must be stopped".

This is not to say that even the cuckiest of cucks is willing to be identified as a cuckservative. Whether they're politicians, journalists, media pundits, consultants, speechwriters, or teleprompter repairmen, conservatives go out of their way to deny the validity of the word as well as the legitimacy of its application to themselves. While they protest the left's most absurd name-calling in a feeble manner, they strike back like raging lions against anyone calling them out for what they truly are. So, as a public service, we offer a field guide to identifying the American cuckservative:

- Refers to leftists as "misguided idealists" or anything even remotely similar, as opposed to something more observably accurate such as "crazy and evil" or "batshit insane".

- Considers socialism to be a "beautiful dream" rather than an economic absurdity.

- Thinks the United States's current problems can be solved by tax cuts for billionaires.

- Believes that the historical culture and political traditions of an immigrant's homeland has absolutely no bearing on that immigrant's future opinions and voting patterns in the United States.

- Insists the Republican Party needs to cater to the preferences of recent Hispanic immigrants to stay relevant.

- Supports immigration reform that includes "a path to citizenship" or amnesty.

- Argues that repatriating immigrants who are here illegally is immoral or racist.

- Supports border security for Israel, but not for the United States.

- Has ever used the phrases "Hispanics are natural conservatives", "family values don't stop at the Rio Grande" or "illegal immigration is an act of love."

- Responds to criticism of immigration or open borders by implying that the critic is racist.

- Asserts that "liberals are the real racists", though never, of course, in the presence of those liberals themselves.

- Demands Americans not give into the fear of terrorism, but give into the fear of being called racist instead.

- Says that Islam means "peace", not "submission".

- Imitates leftists in making fun of working-class whites who fear losing their jobs to immigration or free trade.

- Rides to the defense of a female media figure, no matter how rich, powerful or connected she is, because some boor from outside the Beltway dared to impugn her honor.

- Asserts, contrary to all evidence historical and scientific, that "diversity is our strength".

- Makes a point of speaking regularly in a language other than English in a futile attempt to appeal to whatever constituency speaks that language.

- Is white, but has adopted a non-white child in order to signal virtue to friends and colleagues.

- Claims the word *cuckservative* is racist.

- Insists we should emulate secular European governments by welcoming Muslim refugees on the grounds of Christian charity.

- Sees no difference between an America populated by the inheritors of an ancient Common Law tradition associated with peace, prosperity, and stability, and an America populated by recent arrivals from the world's worst disaster zones.

- Would rather surrender any of his own stated core principles than endure the slightest chance of being called racist.

The above list is far from comprehensive, but should suffice to identify any cuckservatives of one's acquaintance as well as capturing the cuckservative spirit of noble failure. By far the most important identifier on the list is the last one. There is absolutely *nothing* more important to the cuckservative than avoiding being called racist by anyone, particularly by anyone who happens to be black. Sadly for the cuckservative, his prime objective has become increasingly more difficult in recent years, as we are reliably informed that both noticing an individual's race and *not* noticing it are microaggressions that only a shameless racist would commit.

However, while the cuckservative failure has been comprehensive, it cannot be truly said that it has been complete. The cuckservatives have had some degree of success in helping their counterparts on the center-left empower the entire vast control apparatus of the country— the apparatus they began by claiming to oppose—on behalf of big business against the American people. But despite their decades of supplication, the left still openly treats conservatives with sneering contempt while Wall Street supports liberals and Democrats whenever they find it more profitable, so it appears the cuckservatives didn't even get their 30 pieces of silver for betraying America.

Chapter 5

Fifty Years of Failure

This bill we sign today is not a revolutionary bill. It does not affect the lives of millions. It will not restructure the shape of our daily lives.

—President Lyndon Johnson, October 3, 1965

Less prophetic words have seldom been spoken.

Americans tend to assume that the current immigration system, whatever its problems, gradually evolved out of some longstanding tradition or norms. This is not, in fact, the case. This chapter is titled 'fifty years of failure' and not 'two hundred fifty years of failure' for good reason. Something significant changed fifty years prior to the publication of this book. In the midst of an era of unfettered legislation and aggressive expansion of power by the Federal government, it was considered less important at the time than many other laws passed at the time. It is completely forgotten by the general public today, and is rarely mentioned by the political and cultural establishment, yet it completely altered the very complexion of the country. That change was the Hart-Celler Immigration and Nationality Act of 1965.

Even left-leaning Wikipedia says of the act "The 1965 act marked a radical break from the immigration policies of the past."

But what did it replace? What were those policies from which it departed so dramatically? Article I, section 8, clause 4 of the Constitution grants Congress the power to regulate naturalization, the process of a foreigner becoming a citizen. Immigration advocates like to claim this means that the early United States allowed universal and unrestricted immigration. They achieve this by a dishonest semantic sleight-of-hand equating mere entry into the country—the broad category that includes tourism, business travel, and, for that matter, people temporarily stepping off a boat on its way somewhere else to eat or relieve themselves— with permanent immigration. In the era that the country was founded, governments generally lacked the resources or inclination to track every sailor leaving a cargo ship for a night of drinking. Even so, in the United States, laws governing entry existed at the state level from colonial times until the first national regulations were established in 1875.

In fact, very few nations in history have *ever* allowed anyone from anywhere to simply show up and become a citizen. Even tribal societies with no concept of citizenship as such invariably maintain distinctions, often very sharp, between being one of them, a member, or not. Those political entities that *did* allow all comers were those that made no practical distinction between citizen and non-citizen, where all inhabitants (or more often, all except a hereditary aristocracy) were undifferentiated subjects without meaningful rights, and were valuable only as taxpayers or labor. In short, multinational, authoritarian empires.

Congress first exercised its constitutional power to regulate immigration with the Naturalization Act of 1790 which required two years residency, and limited naturalization to white persons of 'good moral character'. The residency requirement was extended to 14 years by 1798, and in 1802 uniform rules were established for the registration of non-citizen residents. In stark contrast to today's looser law, relatives of immigrants were given no particular preference. Even non-citizen wives of citizens were not granted automatic citizenship until 1855, and U.S.-born children of non-citizens were not given such until 1898.

For reasons very specific to the time, other changes were made that may seem impossibly prejudiced and irrational to modern readers, though current immigration law is no more fair or rational. Chinese were specifically excluded from immigration in 1882, Japanese in 1907, and East Indians in 1923. On the other hand, Blacks were specifically granted the right to immigrate in 1870. A literacy requirement for all immigrants was added in 1917. In general, throughout this era, the law continued to favor European immigrants on the reasonable grounds that they were the most compatible with American culture and traditions.

Even with the stricter regulations that were in place, the immigrant population of the United States boomed in the late 19th and early 20th centuries. At the very height of that wave in 1910, 14.7 percent of the U.S. population was foreign-born. Compare this with 13.3 percent, and rapidly rising, in 2014. The overwhelming majority of those immigrants in 1910 were European, and of cultures we today recognize as part of the West. And yet, a foreign population that high led to concern among the native-born population much like we're seeing today.

The result was the Emergency Quota Act of 1921, and its more comprehensive follow-up, the Immigration Act of 1924. The latter put in place nation-of-origin quotas that specifically favored northwest Europe, and a total cap of 170,000 visas per year. Contrary to later spin that the 1924 law represented some unique act of American racism, other nations that had recently been the recipients of massive waves of immigration, including Canada, Brazil, and Argentina, enacted similar national-origin quotas around the same time. Unsurprisingly, the

1921 and 1924 acts inaugurated a 40-year period of significantly lower immigration, and a drop in the foreign-born share of the population to 5.4 percent by 1960.

The first twenty years of that era were marked by boom and then bust, and finally the profound national crucible of the Second World War. The 1920s boom, coinciding as it did with the new regime of more limited immigration, forced employers to find ways to boost productivity besides simply adding more cheap imported labor. Wages rose sharply, and even in the government-induced catastrophes of the 1930s, never fully fell to their old, lower levels. The renewed boom and prosperity that began in the late 1940s, again in an era when employers could not simply add labor from an unlimited supply, correlated with the largest rise in incomes of the largest group of people in human history—the emergence of the modern American middle class.

As we've discussed in prior chapters, America's so-called 'melting pot' was the result of conscious effort. Government at all levels, schools and even community organizations put work into cultural and linguistic assimilation before, after, and especially during the Second World War. During the decades between 1924 and 1965 the children and grandchildren of the immigrants from the prior great wave were absorbed into existing society, and ultimately the modern American identity was forged. Pan-European in its roots, it was and is less skeptical of government power than the Anglo-Saxon culture of the prior era, but it was still recognizably American.

Political lines on immigration were nothing like what they are today. The left was still enthralled with its old Marxist vision of class revolution by an undifferentiated proletariat, and had not yet realized it could pursue a divide-and-conquer strategy against the people themselves, let alone replace them with another, more tractable people. The Democratic Party was vastly more beholden to private-sector blue-collar labor unions than it is today—public-sector unions were in their infancy; there was no large population of fashionably left-wing, self-hating middle-class SWPL whites; modern tribal identity politics, while derived from Marxism, had not yet been invented; and even trial lawyers, prior to the great postwar litigation boom, were a minor force. The other main power base of the Democratic Party were Southern whites, and they were no more in favor of unlimited immigration than blue-collar industrial workers.

On the other side, the old right, rooted in historical Anglo-Saxon American culture, ranged from skeptical to hostile toward further mass immigration. The Republican Party of the time was generally torn between traditionalist and isolationist opposition to more immigration and its own history of pro-business, and thus pro-labor-supply policies. African-Americans at mid-century were actually divided between the two parties, though in transition to the Democrats. The modern regime of mass welfare dependency was not yet in place, and working-class blacks tended to share the same antipathy toward immigrant competition for jobs as working-class whites.

The 1965 act changed all that, along with the very makeup of the country, though prior to its passage, it was not advertised as doing anything of the kind. Nor do most of even its supporters seem to have had any idea how radical it would prove to be. The new law moved U.S. immigration law from a system of differential quotas set by specific nation of origin to one in which every country in the eastern hemisphere had the same equal quota, while the western hemisphere shared a single large quota open to all countries within it. However, all of these would be rendered meaningless by the second main provision of the law—family reunification. Under the reunification system, legal residents could sponsor their relatives for priority treatment, and naturalized citizens could do so *entirely outside the numerical quotas*. Then, those relatives could do the same in turn through a process that came to be known as chain migration.

The last and least, though at the time most-hyped, feature of the new law was a theoretical emphasis on what skills a potential immigrant brought with him. In practice, this proved to be limited to the replacement of the Bracero program of agricultural guest workers from Mexico, which expired in 1964, and the elimination of certain simple general preferences for educated professional immigrants in favor of what became the far more complex current system of specialized business and work visas including H-1B, H-2A, H-2B and D-1.

The motives of those supporting the change in the law weren't uniform, though most were similar to those of immigration advocates today. Emanuel Celler, one of the named co-sponsors of the bill, was a lifelong left-wing internationalist and enemy of traditional American positions ranging from isolationism to gun rights. A congressman since 1923 and a vocal opponent of the 1924 law, he saw victory and vindication in the new bill. Many other supporters considered the law to be part of the broader civil rights movement, and were embarrassed by the overtly ethno-national quotas of the old law. Still others, in the same context, seem to have primarily wanted to avoid being labeled racist. Even so, proponents of the bill made great effort to downplay its possible demographic effects on the future United States:

> *Out of deference to the critics, I want to comment on ... what the bill will not do. First, our cities will not be flooded with a million immigrants annually. Under the proposed bill, the present level of immigration remains substantially the same ... Secondly, the ethnic mix of this country will not be upset ... Contrary to the charges in some quarters, S.500 will not inundate America with immigrants from any one coun-*

try or area, or the most populated and economically deprived nations of Africa and Asia.

—Senator Edward Kennedy (D-MA)

This bill is not designed to increase or accelerate the number of newcomers permitted to come to America. This bill would retain all the present security and health safeguards of the present law. The overall effect of this bill on employment would, first of all, be negligible, and second, that such effect as might be felt would not be harmful, but beneficial. The actual net increase in total immigration under this bill would be about 60,000. Those immigrants who seek employment are estimated at a maximum of 24,000. Our present labor force, however, is 77 million. Statistically or practically, we are talking about an infinitesimal amount."

—United States Attorney General Nicholas Katzenbach

...while the national origins rule will be eliminated in establishing quotas for foreign countries, this does not mean that the bill would permit a flood tide of new immigrants into this country. As a matter of fact, the total number of potential immigrants would not be changed very much."

—Senator Daniel K. Inouye (D-HI)

These grand claims were made proactively and defensively. At the time, public opinion was not in favor of the Act. A Harris poll of May 1965 showed 58 percent of the public was opposed to easing immigration law, with only 24 percent in favor. Nevertheless, politicians who dared to oppose the law were scarce. Most of those who dared do so were Southern Democrats, answerable to their traditionalist, socially conservative base. A handful of others were Republicans of the still-new conservative movement, though many of their more proto-cuckservative peers fled for cover after the defeats and divisions of the prior two years. Only Senator Sam Ervin of North Carolina, a Democrat not part of the conservative movement, had the courage to argue against the bill at length, and on unashamed nationalist and historical grounds:

> *Mr. Secretary ... do you know of any people in the world that have contributed more to making America than those particular groups? ... In other words, you take the English-speaking people, they gave us our language, they gave us our common law, they gave us a large part of our political philosophy.... The reason I say this bill is discriminatory against those people is because it puts them on exactly the same plane as the people of Ethiopia are put, where the people of Ethiopia have the same right to come to the United States under this bill as the people from England, the people of France, the people of Germany, the people of Holland, and I don't think ... I don't know of any contributions that Ethiopia has made to the making of America.*

In reply to claims that the old laws were discriminatory, but the new law would not be, he elaborated:

> *I do not think you could draft an immigration bill in which you do not discriminate. I think discrimination is ordinarily the exercise of intelligence to make conscious choices.... we always discriminate, only the basis of it is different, each of us think[s] our own way is wise and right.... I think there is a rational basis and a reasonable basis to give a preference to Holland over Afghanistan*

For this, Ervin and the few who stood with him were pilloried in the press, and their observations were treated as being on roughly the same plane as belief in a flat earth. The *Washington Post* and the then-popular *Saturday Evening Post* equated the old national-origins system to Jim Crow laws in the South. Edward Kennedy implied that critics of the proposed bill were both bigots and un-American:

> *The charges I have mentioned are highly emotional, irra-tional, and with little foundation in fact. They are out of line with the obligations of responsible citizenship. They breed hate of our heritage.*

Republican Senator Hiram Fong of Hawaii went even farther, and offered support for the law via an unusual explanation for the Second World War, one that strangely foreshadowed modern rationalizations for Islamic terror attacks:

> *"One of the reasons why the United States was attacked, on December 7, 1941, was because of these exclusionary laws [the 1924 Immigration Act] which had fomented so much bad feeling between the peoples of Japan and the United States."*

By contrast, the *New York Times* attempted a less confrontational, loftier, and more vacuous linkage of the proposed law to the Civil Rights movement:

> *...no piece of legislation [Hart-Celler] before Congress that in terms of decency and equity is more demanding of passage. In a time when this country is attempting to wipe away an-cient wrongs against its Negro citizens, its conscience will not permit a sign at all ports of entry reading: 'Only whites from Northwestern Europe are welcome.'*

While the astute reader might have a hard time understanding how opening the gates to immigrants from Cambodia or Ecuador would right any ancient wrongs against native-born blacks, particularly since they would all soon be in direct competition with each other for jobs, no doubt the wise sages at the *New York Times* had their reasons.

Though today obscured by decades of leftist narrative and media spin about Republican racism, the bill was passed with a larger percentage of support (85 percent) from Republicans than Democrats (74 percent) in Congress. As with most complex and controversial legislation, the actual implementation of the 1965 act was set for several years later, in this case 1968, and its effects were not felt in earnest until the early 1970s.

One of the more immediate effects of the law resulted from a curious loophole. While countries in the eastern Hemisphere each had nominal quotas of 20,000 immigrants per year, the western Hemisphere had a combined quota of 120,000 with no cap by country. This naturally weighted the influx in favor of America's southern neighbor, Mexico. The latter had nearly doubled in population between 1940 and 1960, while remaining economically stagnant, and its population would nearly triple again between 1960 and 2000. Proximity, poverty, and large extended families combined with the chain migration system to dramatically boost legal immigration from Mexico in the 1970s. At the same time, the end of the Bracero program, laxer enforcement of border security, and widespread support by agricultural and business interests combined to hugely increase *illegal* immigration.

Another consequence of the law stemmed from the family preferences system. It tended to favor both more recent immigrants with families still overseas, and those from societies with larger, better-knit extended families and clans, as well as those, frankly, more comfortable with nepotism. As such, it actually began to discriminate against some older U.S. ethnic groups, just as Sen. Ervin had predicted.

As average annual immigration grew to 450,000 in the 1970s and 740,000 in the 1980s, the public began to notice, and pressure grew for Congress to do something. In time they certainly did, and with bipartisan support, it proved to be something very bad. In 1986 comprehensive immigration reform was added under a name of Orwellian irony, the Immigration Reform and Control Act, or IRCA. In terms that will sound drearily familiar to today's readers, it proposed a general amnesty and a path to citizenship for some 3.8 million illegal immigrants without otherwise significant criminal records in the United States, in return for supposed increases in border security and enforcement. As with every subsequent amnesty and call for amnesty, this was supposed to be one to end them all.

In the end, the IRCA benefits program ran on for more than twenty-five years, ultimately granting amnesty to some 3 million of the 3.8 million candidates. However, IRCA beneficiaries who became citizens went on to invite, at a minimum, over 740,000 immediate relatives under the Hart-Celler family unification preferences. When those whom the relatives in turn invited are counted, along with other beneficiaries of the family preference system, the number of add-on immigrants resulting from the amnesty was likely as high as 1.9 million. Thus in total, IRCA by itself added some 4.9 million new Americans, nearly all of them from Mexico. As with many other large Federal benefits programs, the IRCA was riddled with fraud, and as many as a quarter of applications came from illegals who didn't actually meet the requirements of the law—making them illegal aliens trying to become legal in an illegal manner.

Unfortunately, the promised increases in border security and enforcement never quite happened. The immigration enforcement budget was increased, as it continued to be in subsequent years, until by 2012 it had reached fifteen times its inflation-adjusted 1986 level. Yet then as now, the immigration enforcers had their own priorities as to the uses of that money. Even regarding the problem of fraud within the IRCA itself, the Immigration and Naturalization Service chose to transfer at least $50 million in funds from fraud prevention to such pressing needs as new computers for INS administrators. The IRCA introduced the famous I-9 form, familiar to new job applicants in the United States, but the latter remains to this day a self-verified document that generally ends up buried in employee files rather than providing any data to anyone.

On the other hand, cuckservative Republicans and even President Reagan himself received the occasional positive stroking from the press at the time, so there was that.

The IRCA set the pattern for all subsequent immigration 'reform' of the next thirty years, including the relatively major effort of the Immigration Act of 1990, the impressively-named Illegal Immigration Reform and Immigrant Responsibility Act of 1996, the various smaller amnesties of the 1990s, and the REAL ID Act of 2005. The various versions of 'comprehensive immigration reform' passed around in the last ten years have, nearly all, been faintly warmed-over remakes of the IRCA. Meanwhile, immigration numbers, both legal and illegal, continued to climb.

Debate follows the same patterns it did with IRCA as well, though the paths are a lot more worn now, and the carpet is getting threadbare. Nearly every year, the same predictable show returns, though the actors might be a bit more tired. Cuckservatives will meekly appear, egged on by their wealthy donors, and propose theoretical enforcement accompanied by a very real amnesty. Leftists will leap, trundle, or sometimes prance onto the stage and angrily demand amnesty without any pesky enforcement. Open-borders libertarians, for as little as they matter, will put on their Milton Friedman hats and 1970s supply-side leisure

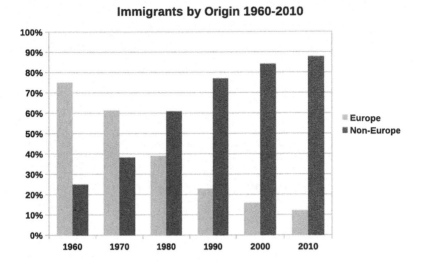

Figure 5.1: Immigrants by Origin 1960–2010

suits, and then sing their traditional lounge songs about the fantastic economic benefits of unlimited immigration. If anyone gets bored, old Uncle Joe Biden will show up, pass out cocktails, slap a few backs, and maybe pinch a few backsides.

Yet while the show goes on, same as always, the country itself has been changing fast. The original backers of the 1965 Immigration Act were confident, even condescending, in their assurances to skeptics that things would largely proceed as before. Census statistics from 1960 to 2010 concerning the countries of origin from which the New Americans emigrated reveal just how catastrophically false those assurances were.

This is an incredible transformation, especially for a law that was supposed to add only a few tens of thousands of additional immigrants per year. The promises that the demographic makeup of the post-1965 immigrants would remain the same as before proved entirely false.

While part of the change may be attributed to the fact that improving economic conditions in Europe made emigration to America less relatively attractive, that does not mean it was beneficial for America to replace it with immigration from non-European nations. Only in the fantasies of leftists and cuckservatives is a Somali militiaman just as capable of becoming an American as an English shopkeeper.

As it happens, the raw number of immigrants from Europe has actually been increasing since the 1990s, but it is still declining as a percentage of all immigrants due to the steadily rising number of immigrants from the third world.

This long-term flood of immigrants is fundamentally altering everything about American society, including the very language we speak. The Center for Immigration Studies put the number of *native-born* U.S. citizens speaking something other than English at home at 25.9 million in 2010. This is significant, especially when one considers that only a quarter of the countries on Earth have populations that large; non-English speakers make up a separate nation-within-a-nation that is larger than Australia. Meanwhile, the total number of residents, whether citizens or not, speaking Spanish at home was estimated by the U.S. Census Bureau at 38.4 million for 2013. If that population were its own country, it would be the 8th largest Spanish-speaking nation in the world.

Cuckservatives, naturally, see no problem with this. Some even go so far as to claim that they would illegally immigrate themselves.

Many people who came here illegally are doing exactly what we would do if we lived in a country where we couldn't feed our families. If my kids went to sleep hungry every night and my country didn't give me an opportunity to feed them, there isn't a law, no matter how restrictive, that would prevent me from coming here.

—Marco Rubio, *An American Son*, 2012

Cuckservatives have also long conceded the moral high ground on immigration, even on *illegal immigration*, to the left. While they'll get teary-eyed with weepy emotionalism when discussing immigrants and their contributions, when discussing border security and the need to keep track of illegal aliens they tend to fall back on cold and technical analysis, or vague generalities about securing the border. Either way, they fold in a crisis. Cuckservative pundit, churchian Mormon, and former immigration semi-skeptic Glenn Beck collapsed into a puddle of abject apologetic submission during 2014's unusually large wave of illegal immigrant children:

> *I know what I have said in the past was controversial. Some of it foolish, some of it wrong, some of it poorly worded. But on the same page, some of it right and some of it needed to be said. For those things that were said by me that caused needless division, I am deeply sorry.*

—Glenn Beck, July 4, 2014

For its part, the Obama administration, frustrated with the annual Congressional immigration show, has followed its preferred route of unilateral executive action. From the beginning of his first term, Obama officials began to interpret the restrictions on entry into the United States considerably more loosely than had the previous administration. The number of border cards and visas of all types issued has nearly doubled, from 5.8 million to 9.9 million, while the rejection rate has declined from 18.6 percent to 15.3 percent.

Perhaps eager to emulate the success and popularity of the 2015 EU refugee program, as championed by German Chancellor Merkel, the Obama administration has also announced plans to admit more than 12,000 refugees from Syria to the United States. The President accompanied his plan with threats, including the termination of Federal funding, to state and local governments that fail to comply, and offered the following heartwarming comparison of Syrian factional fighters to some of the original settlers of what became the United States:

> *"Nearly four centuries after the Mayflower set sail, the world is still full of pilgrims—men and women who want nothing more than the chance for a safer, better future for themselves and their families. What makes America America is that we offer that chance."*

—President Barack Hussein Obama, November 26, 2015

In response, cuckservatives complained that not all the presumed refugees were Syrian and that they couldn't be properly vetted, while simultaneously engaging in their own virtue signaling regarding the refugees. No doubt these complaints will work as well as quibbling about the technical details has with other administration decisions over the past six years.

Immigration advocates often claim that immigrants not only work harder, or at least hold more jobs, than native-born citizens, but that they actually draw on fewer government benefits, or when that seems less convincing, that they at least pay more in taxes than they receive in benefits. And while the data supports some of their claims, the net conclusion is far from favorable.

It is true that immigrant households are more likely to be employed than native-born households, 87 to 76 percent, although since effectively all the new jobs created since 2009 have gone to immigrants, it is not exactly an argument in favor of bringing in even more. However, immigrant households are also much more likely to be on some form of welfare, 51 percent to 28 percent. This means that at least 38 percent of immigrant households are simultaneously bringing in money from both jobs and welfare. This is a higher percentage than all native-born households receiving welfare. And compounding the problem, immigrant households also pay 11 percent less in taxes per dollar earned.

In other words, if you want citizens who pay less in taxes, but receive more government spending than the ones you already have, by all means, import more.

But without question the worst effect caused by 50 years of failure, and the one most likely to have the most severe long-term consequences, is the negative effect immigration has had on the collective national intelligence. Researchers around the world have observed that the nations of the West have been gradually becoming less intelligent; the Danish military measured a 1.5 point decline in the average IQ of its soldiers between 1998 and 2014, while the average British 14-year-old lost two IQ points from 1980 to 2008. The same is true for the USA, where a three-point average IQ gain that took place after the Melting Pot migration ended has been entirely reversed as a result of immigration from lower-IQ nations.

By multiplying the average measured IQs for the four major ethnic groups in the United States with their changing demographic ratios, we can calculate how the demographic changes have affected the national intelligence over time. In 1960, we calculate the national IQ average to have been 100.3. By 2010, the average national IQ had fallen four points, to 96. By 2030, if the current population estimates are correct, it will fall another point, to 95. Lest you think that average national intelligence is irrelevant, note that just that four-point difference is essentially equal to the difference between countries such as Austria, the

Netherlands, and the United Kingdom, and countries such as Uruguay and Portugal. There is a strong correlation between societal wealth and average national intelligence as measured in IQ.

Even the left-wing British paper, the *Guardian*, was recently forced to take note of this phenomenon, as it reported that scientists have determined genes influence academic ability across all subjects, and that as much as 60 percent of the observed differences between various population groups can be explained by genetic factors. So, the mass migration of the last 50 years has been materially dysgenic and has literally made Americans stupider on average. It's not just you, mass entertainment really has been dumbed down in recent decades in order to appeal to what is an even lower common denominator than before.

Whatever one thinks of these changes, this is one of the fastest demographic transformations of a nation in recorded human history, and it is the direct result of public policy. This changing reality is also changing the public mood. Public polls for decades have shown broad support for immigration in the abstract, but as the unexpectedly successful presidential campaigns of the more immigration-skeptical candidates has shown, that historical support is shallow and very subject to change. Aware of the growing weaknesses in their positions, in recent years some open-immigration advocates have resorted to a new argument: since border control is impossible, why bother?

> *Billions of dollars are wasted annually in a futile effort to seal an inherently unsealable border. More people have died trying to cross over from Mexico in the past decade than were killed on Sept. 11. Ever tougher measures won't work: Documents can be forged or stolen, people smuggled, officials bribed. Even with a shoot-to-kill policy, people got across the Berlin Wall.*

—Philippe Legrain, *Forbes*, June 10, 2010

Mexican border crossings and the 9/11 attacks are a spectacularly unrelated apples-and-oranges comparison, but the Berlin Wall is a slightly more apt comparison, if inverted. Legrain states people got across the Berlin Wall. Indeed they did; all 4,950 of them in the 28 years of its existence, or if we play loosely and use the entire East-West German border, 40,100 people. Meanwhile, in the 11 years *before* the wall and the fences went up, 3.45 *million* people escaped from East Germany to the West.

It must be admitted the German problem was one of emigration, quite the reverse of America's immigration concerns, but for border security forces the challenge was much the same—people moving across a line they were not permitted to cross. The real difference was in the will to do something, a will that was ruthlessly present in East German leaders charged with enforcing an evil, totalitarian system, and totally lacking in American leaders responsible for defending a free society.

Chapter 6

The Madness of Open Borders

Arabs are Arabs, the French are French. Do you think the French body politic can absorb ten million Muslims, who tomorrow will be twenty million, after tomorrow forty? If we integrated, if all the Arabs and Berbers of Algeria were considered French, would you prevent them to settle in France, where the standard of living is so much higher? My village would no longer be called Colombey-The-Two-Churches but Colombey-The-Two-Mosques.

—Charles de Gaulle, March 5, 1959

Imagine yourself affluent and established, in a prosperous if not lavishly wealthy neighborhood. You have a family, a nice house, a small guest room over your garage, and a yard even bigger than the most famous expanse of green in science fiction. One morning you find a bedraggled man camped on your front lawn. At first you consider calling the police on him, but in the end decide to simply go outside and ask him to leave. But when you talk to him, you learn that he is out of work and is now homeless. He mentions he has some experience as a landscaper and handyman, and he offers to do some work around your property in return for spending the night in your guest room. After some initial reluctance, you reflect on your own good fortune and decide that perhaps it wouldn't be the worst thing in the world to let him stay. It seems a small imposition, especially when you have so much and there are a few things that need doing around the place. In the end, you agree.

To your surprise, he does a fantastic job. He mows, weeds, and trims all over your grounds, then spends half the night doing minor repairs in the guest room itself. You bring him breakfast, and as you look over his handiwork, he asks if it would be a problem if he stayed a few more nights. While you never would have agreed to an extended stay in the first place, now you're so impressed with his work that you decide to grant his request. For the next week, everything goes well. By the weekend, he has the yard looking immaculate, he's repainted the exterior of the garage, and has even repaired the roof on the old storage shed at the back of the property. You're so impressed that you agree when he asks if it is all right if he stays for the summer. You've gotten used to having him around, and it's kind of nice to have someone to have a beer with in the evenings.

Another week passes, and your trust in your new guest has grown to the point that you've let him join the family for lunch on a couple of occasions. One day, however, you visit the guest room and find a strange woman there. She's got a baby with her. You ask her who she is, and she explains she's your guest's wife, who's been staying in a shelter while her husband worked for you. The man returns, apologizes for the confusion, and asks if she can stay. He suggests that his wife might be able to help out as a housekeeper. You eye the innocent baby, feeling sorry for the poor thing, and despite your better judgment, you tell him they can stay.

Halfway through the third week, you notice the once-homeless man now has an assistant helping him around the property. The new guy speaks only broken English. Your guest explains that this is his cousin, a refugee from the war-torn, impoverished country he escaped as a child. He suggests his cousin could help him, but you point out that the man and his wife are already doing about as much work as needs to be done around the place. He then suggests that his cousin could work for your neighbors for cash, and pay you a small rent for being permitted to stay in the guest room with him. The cousin is a thin, pitiful-looking fellow, half a head shorter than his American-raised relative. Again, you find yourself giving in.

Another week later and your guest's wife's sister has arrived. She has three children. They too have a sad story. You have no work for them, but they find it around the neighborhood, and offer you a little more rent. The guest room is packed now, but feeling guilty over the idea of the kids sleeping in the garage, you let the sister and her children stay in a spare bedroom of the main house. Your younger child is delighted to have playmates, but the older one is upset because the new children not only outnumber yours, but keep leaving his toys scattered around the house and breaking them.

More time passes, and new relatives arrive, along with acquaintances of uncertain origins. They fill up both the garage and all the extra rooms in your home. Fortunately, the old storage shed has been repaired, so some of the newcomers move in there. Most of them pay you some sort of rent, although at this point, even your neighbors don't have enough work for them all. Some make money from outside jobs, or by setting up little shops on your property. At least one appears to have turned to stealing though, as you notice small things start to go missing around your house.

As time passes, more and more people arrive. With no more space indoors, they have begun hammering makeshift houses together in your back yard. Few of them speak English, you don't know their names, and they begin throwing raucous, drunken parties. Sometimes there are even fights that are disturbingly violent. Trash and waste are beginning to pile up everywhere. You begin to feel that perhaps things are getting a little out of control. Your friend, an economics professor, notes approvingly that you're making a lot of extra money from all the rent, and with so many people, you get their labor almost for free. In fact, he even tells you that if your property were a country, it would have grown enormously in terms of both population and economic output.

This is true, so far as it goes. Yet when you look around you and see all the people and the squalor and the trash and the violence, you suddenly realize that your home is no longer your own.

Soon your neighbors start to complain. They tell you of cars being stolen, of properties being vandalized, and of friends who lost their jobs because newcomers were willing to do the same work for a lot less money. Some of your old neighbors move away, and large groups of new people take their places in the recently vacated houses. Their behavior is even worse than the people who are living in your house, and your garage, and your shed, and your lawn. One day, the original homeless man, his wife and child at his side, comes to speak with you. He thanks you for everything you've done for him, but he says that things have gotten too crowded and unsafe on your property, so he and his family are leaving for somewhere better. However, everyone who followed him, everyone else, they'll be staying put, with you.

The story may be fanciful, but it is exactly what open borders and near-unlimited immigration mean for America, or for any other Western country sufficiently wealthy and attractive to be deemed an immigration destination by the inhabitants of less successful societies.

Consider another, less fantastical situation. Suppose you were applying for a job. The position requires specialized skills, which you fortunately possess, and jobs of this kind usually pay about twice the average wage for your city. Normally, you'd compete for the job against a local pool of qualified applicants. Now imagine two alternative scenarios. In the first, you are the only qualified applicant anywhere nearby. This is great for you, but less so for the company. Since you have no competition to drive down the price of your labor, you might be able to negotiate an unusually high rate of pay. And, ego aside, you might or might not actually be the best person for the job. If they have strong enough doubts about you, or you get too greedy negotiating for your salary, they might even go through the extra effort and expense to recruit further applicants from outside the area. Regardless, the company will likely try to charge more to cover your additional cost, or cut their costs elsewhere. Libertarians will readily point out the economic disadvantages of this unbalanced scenario, yet they generally love the following, equally unbalanced situation.

In the second scenario, you are in direct competition with hundreds of people from around the world for the same position. In one country, the government subsidizes the training needed for this kind of job, so there is a huge glut of qualified but unemployed applicants. In another, the government followed disastrous policies that ruined the economy, and applicants with your skills are now desperate for any work whatsoever. Numerous applicants from both countries either are already here, or can easily get here. This is obviously great for the company, which can hire what they at least think will be the best candidate out of a much larger pool. And with so many applicants competing for the same position, they can pay drastically less too. It is wonderful in abstract economic terms, but you, personally, are now likely out of a job.

The cuckservative establishment certainly agrees it would be a good thing. Of course they prefer to phrase it in generalities about economic benefits, with perhaps a bit of watery patriotism thrown in:

> *And good policy on immigration in the United States is, we are in a global battle for capital and labor, and we need to have what is good economic policy for America on immigration because we do need labor. We not only need Ph.Ds in science and technology, we need skilled workers and we need unskilled workers. And we need to have an immigration policy that is good economic policy, and then—and then the politics will take care of itself.*

—Gov. Haley Barbour, Mississippi, November 8, 2012

From Gov. Barbour's comments, one might think that in 2012, the superheated United States economy was experiencing drastic labor shortages, as opposed to say, the lowest labor force participation rate in more than thirty years (and which has continued to decline since). However, the unstated qualifier of his references to labor and workers is 'cheap'. An influx of cheaper foreign labor, both skilled and unskilled, would in fact be good for the economy in macro terms, though of course not so much for individual laborers. It would also indeed be beneficial in the global competition for capital, in the sense of putting more of it into the hands of his friends and donors.

Some economic theorists, usually libertarians with some sort of academic tenure, are more bluntly honest:

A policy of open immigration would indeed force unskilled American laborers to compete for their jobs at lower wages. However, far from being an evil, this is a desirable outcome, one which should form the basis for a new immigration policy. By inviting competition into the American labor markets, artificially inflated labor costs could be eliminated and a greater level of labor efficiency could be achieved.

—Prof. Thomas E. Lehman, Foundation for Economic Education, December 1, 1995

How comforting that Professor Lehman assures us only unskilled workers, who presumably don't matter, would see their "artificially inflated" wages reduced. However, the effects of unlimited competition for jobs have affected vast numbers of middle-class workers in the years since he wrote those words. In just one very recent example, favorable immigration treatment for tech workers, bolstered by the H-1B and other temporary visa programs, has allowed the technology industry, including tech giants Intel, Microsoft, and Qualcomm, to fire tens of thousands of American employees and replace them on American soil with recently imported foreigners for far lower pay. Keep in mind, *each and every time* you see one of these arguments, that unless you're a large corporate employer yourself, *you* are the 'artificially inflated labor cost' they want to reduce through immigrant-imported competition.

Realizing that the above might not be a popular position, other open-borders advocates use less direct economic arguments, rhetorical leaps, or emotionally-manipulative soundbites based on the wonderful magic of importing talented human capital. And some make comments that are so overtly stupid they are facepalm-worthy:

Every visa officer today lives in fear that he will let in the next

> *Mohammed Atta. As a result, he is probably keeping out the*
> *next Bill Gates.*
>
> —Fareed Zakaria, *The Washington Post*,
> November 23, 2004

Ignoring the *slight* problem that Bill Gates is, in fact, a native-born American citizen, to say nothing of the fact that Mohammed Atta was not an immigrant either, but actually entered the country on a five-year tourist/business visa, Zakaria's ridiculous statement omits the obvious point that the immigration debate has never been about the handful of people who are freakishly rare outliers on the bell curve of human achievement, but about the tens of millions of people who are not. Moreover, the vast majority of immigrants today are coming from nations with an average intelligence level that is considerably lower than that of the American citizenry, in some cases more than a standard deviation lower.

Yet increased competition for jobs is only a small fragment of the huge societal problems that open borders would inevitably inspire. Comparatively prosperous, peaceful, stable Western nations possess an appeal that extends far beyond jobs. Most immigrants want to come to the United States simply to escape the crime and poverty of their own countries, in the hopes of living off of government benefits, or even to live like the Kardashians. They watch U.S. television, which gives them an extremely skewed notion of what life in America is like. And a very great many potential immigrants would like to enjoy life in the wealthy and glamorous land they see on TV.

According to a global Gallup poll of more than 452,000 foreigners, conducted between 2009 and 2012, roughly 14 percent of adults worldwide would like to permanently immigrate to another country if they could. Of those, fully *150 million* would choose the United States.

That number, which could easily be an undercount in practice, takes no account of children or dependent spouses. Another Gallup poll of over 141,000 people did not specify destination by country, but found that fully 26 percent of the world's adults would be willing to migrate temporarily to another country for work. It is possible to estimate what that number means for the United States. Assuming the same distribution of destination countries as among the permanent immigrants, some 279 million adults worldwide would migrate to the United States at least temporarily. Interestingly, this latter study found that would-be temporary migrants skewed more toward educated workers, the kind who would compete directly with the middle class in their destination countries.

Try to imagine the United States suddenly increasing in population by 50 percent or 100 percent. In abstract libertarian economic terms, it would be fantastic. Large companies would appreciate all that additional labor—available so cheaply, and also helpfully driving down the price of native-born labor. With lower labor costs, corporate profits would increase, thus putting more capital in the hands of investors. Landlords and developers would be happy too. The rapid influx of so many new consumers of housing, competing for the much more slowly-growing available stock, would dramatically drive up average rents and new property prices. Thus, along with ridding itself of artificially-inflated labor costs, the country's economy would at last be freed of artificially-low housing costs compared with much of the world.

It is true that immigrants and migrants would need additional goods and services, such as food, clothing, and housing. Those in favor of open borders argue that this gives immigration a kind of multiplier effect, creating more new jobs via increased demand than the immigrants themselves actually fill. This is not, as will be shown in the next chapter, actually true. For the moment, consider what limits there might be on the economic benefits of an unlimited supply of illiterate unskilled laborers, or of a million native-born workers being suddenly replaced by an equal number of recently arrived foreign workers, at half the previous wages.

In addition to the usual economic arguments, open-borders advocates often make a number of non-economic, moral arguments in favor of their cause. Depending on the speaker or writer, those arguments may be libertarian, social-justice leftist, or pseudo-Christian Cuckservative.

One of the most interesting libertarian positions is the so-called Right to Migrate, which holds that moving to and living wherever one pleases is a fundamental right akin to freedom of contract and freedom from coercion. Curiously, like many leftist theories, this idea treats national citizenship itself as meaningless, disposable, and entirely determined by the State. Thus, it makes no distinction between restraining one's citizens from leaving, as totalitarian states do, and preventing some other country's citizens from *entering*. In other words, open-borders theorists see an inhabitant of Pakistan as having just as much right to live in the United States as a lifelong American taxpayer. As a corollary, the American taxpayer, whether on his own or via his government, has no right to prevent the Pakistani from moving in. This summary is not an exaggeration:

> *Preventing you from crossing the border to see your friend, or preventing them from coming to visit you, is no more justifiable than the government erecting roadblocks around a church or other private gathering place to prevent people from meeting there.*

—Grant Babcock, *Libertarianism.org*, October 16, 2014

Consider that for a moment. Notice how carefully it is phrased—'You' being the immigrant in the more memorable first clause, as if we were discussing emigration to Papua New Guinea instead of immigration to a developed country, and note the choice of the word 'friend'. Notice the cosmopolitan, yet naïve, attitude that there is no distinction between visiting a neighbor for coffee, and someone coming to live and work in another country, and no more difference between those neighbors than between two people from opposite sides of the world. Of course, relatively few people hold the above view in such a complete form—for example, few of them would be eager to have *their* neighborhood become a squatter camp—but as a fuzzy, emotional, unstated assumption it underpins plenty of immigration discussion today.

Leftists, for their part, don't generally discuss rights in the sense of being left alone to do something, but in the sense of entitlements to something someone else already has. Who exactly they think is entitled to what has always been a divisive topic on the left, since they know for someone to get, someone else has to be forced to give. More nationalist or communitarian leftists, like mid-20th-century union organizers, 1990s anti-globalization protesters, or Bernie Sanders today, may be skeptical of unlimited immigration, but utopian internationalists see immigration as an extension of their broader campaigns of wealth redistribution and social justice:

> *I find it bizarre that so many people focus on the plight of the least well-off in rich societies, and yet ignore the issue of immigration. From my point of view, if you do not advocate open immigration, any claim to be concerned about social justice or the well being of the poor is mere pretense.*

—Jason Brennan, *The Ethics of Voting*, 2011

Let that sink in. According to this Professor of Philosophy at Georgetown University, who is described as a left-libertarian, any random impoverished person, anywhere in the world, has a right to claim some share in your wealth, and a right to come to your country in order to get it. And, even more remarkably, he thinks it is bizarre if you happen to have a problem with that. One can't help but wonder if he has the same perspective with regards to his personal wealth.

Brennan's isn't the only radical position. Just as supporters of the 1965 Hart-Celler Immigration Act equated the older laws with domestic Jim Crow legislation, some immigration advocates have declared the very existence of national borders to be racist and equivalent to South Africa's now-defunct system of apartheid:

> To be sure, there are differences between the global system of immigration restrictions and South Africa's attempt to entrench white privilege through the partitioning of its territory. But it should give us pause to think that when the architects of one of history's most recognized evils set out to codify their system of injustice, they looked at our borders and passports and saw a lot to like. Intentions aside, the biggest difference between the two is that the South Africans wanted to draw the boundaries and assign the nationalities. We make do with the existing ones.
>
> —Stephan Faris, *Homelands: The Case for Open Immigration*, 2014

That's right, in the name of social justice, it is evil for you, living, working, and paying taxes in your native land, to keep out anyone, from anywhere in the world, who might want to show up and claim a piece of your labor. The boundary that keeps out 150 million, or 275 million, or a billion new neighbors, none of whom lifted a finger to help build your country, is exactly the same as the system under which native-born Africans were forcibly displaced from their own historical lands. Unlike the libertarian economists, Brennan, Faris and those like them harbor no illusions that any of this would be for your benefit.

Traumatic as the arrival of hundreds of millions of new neighbors might be for the average American worker and taxpayer, leftists themselves would be, at least initially, delighted at the dramatic increase in diversity combined with the simultaneous dilution of evil white, English-speaking, Christian, gun-owning culture. Ethnic identity activists of many sorts would suddenly find themselves with considerably more potential political muscle, to support whatever nation-destroying projects they might have in mind.

However, for libertarian and leftist idealists, open borders is an exercise in abstract philosophical perfection. It is an opportunity for them to signal virtue and demonstrate their moral and intellectual superiority over plebs and hicks who might be upset at the mere grubby reality of having to share their paycheck with the entire world, or compete for their job with a hundred competitors willing to work for half the pay. Let alone such backwards wrongthink as preferring to deal in English in a historically English-speaking country. And thinking that there might be some, say, deep-rooted reasons why countries founded by English-speaking Anglo-Saxons are so prosperous and peaceful when so many others continue to not be... well that's just racist.

Some open-borders advocates have actually thought through the implications of a multicultural America of between 500 million and one billion residents, and the few that remained open-borders advocates afterward are those that have been willing to accept some remarkably harsh consequences. The following quote is the longest in this book, but it is worth reading for its unusual honesty:

I would tentatively envision the U.S. experience under open borders as resembling the British and Roman cases, inasmuch as the protocols and ideals of the U.S. polity, as well as its merely ethnic characteristics, would persist in attenuated form, but governing a much larger population would necessitate improvisational and sometimes authoritarian expedients that would cumulatively transform the polity into something quite different, even as it claimed descent from the historic constitutional polity of the United States as we know it. The illusion of continuity would deceive the subjects of the new polity, native-born and immigrant, to a considerable extent, though on the other hand there would be a good deal of lamentation and triumphalism, and only after several generations would historians be able to look back and assess the bewildering transformation in a sober, balanced way.

Certain American ideals would die of their own increasing impracticality, e.g., "equality of opportunity," the social safety net, one person, one vote, or non-discrimination in employment. Americans might continue to feel that these ideals were right long after they had ceased to be practiced, as the Romans seemed to feel that Rome ought to be governed by its Senate long after real governance had passed to the emperors.

—Nathan Smith, *Openborders.info*, August 14, 2015

Many points stated plainly above are left unstated by others—either in guilty denial or implicit approval. The America that emerges in Smith's hypothetical scenario, with undifferentiated subjects, having little to no rights and held together by authoritarian rule, is exactly the type of nation we mentioned early in Chapter 5—the only kind that has historically allowed completely open borders. Comparison with Rome is unfortunately apt, since the Roman state over its history was characterized by ever-wider extension of citizenship, and eventually dilution of the meaning of that citizenship. Rome is also arguably most famous for falling, as have all nations that became multicultural empires.

For others, of course, the above long-term consequences are more than acceptable, and any idealistic abstractions provide no more than a moral cover for their own eminently realistic and immediate interests. The powers-that-be in Washington would be overjoyed to find that instead of facing a more-or-less linguistically cohesive and often resistant native majority, they could work with something far more divided, and thus easier to rule. Some, like the political machine behind President Obama's electoral campaigns, have already proven adept at parsing ever smaller slices of an increasingly diverse electorate for their use and advantage. And unlike many open-borders idealists, the power wielders would be and will continue to be delighted for years to come, since they have armed security and gated communities to keep all that new-found diversity at a safe distance.

And where are the cuckservatives in all this? Where are the thoughtful, earnest defenders of tradition and the American way? Where are those who, by their own self-designation, claim to want to *conserve* something? The complete failure of their immigration policy, and their abject acceptance of the rapid demographic transformation of the United States on the part of cuckservative Republicans has already been discussed. Unfortunately, the cuckservative habit of self-hatred, abasement, apologies and guilt extends into discussions of borders and immigration in general.

> *We Americans, what exactly did we do to earn our prosperity, our freedom? Well, for most of us, what we did was: be born... There is no historical basis for any American to claim*

*the moral high ground when talking about Mexican immi-
gration to the United States. Sure, those wars happened long
ago. But how different do you think the history of Mexico
might have been if all that Texas oil and all that California
gold had stayed within the boundaries of Mexico, as by right
they should have?*

—Orson Scott Card, June 25, 2006

This is a nominal conservative taking the unusual position that you have no particular right to your own country or its traditions, but by some never-stated principle, people from other countries *do*. His reference to the 1840s Mexican-American War invokes the same double standard leftists use, wherein any historical changes in the favor of Europe or the United States are considered to be illegitimate, while changes that worked against them are somehow deemed valid. Also, we propose as a counterpoint to Mr. Card that, on the basis of the historical evidence rather than his very active imagination, the history of Mexico would likely be about what it has been, no matter what additional resources it might have possessed.

That Mexico in particular is also home to the ethno-mythical ideology of *Aztlan*, *la Raza Cósmica*, the racial superiority of mestizos, and the eventual *Reconquista* of the American Southwest is a very different matter, but it is not exactly one that should inspire much naïve idealism about immigration.

But who knows... Orson Scott Card is considered a conservative, but he's just one man, and a science-fiction writer at that, so maybe he's just an oddball? Let's see what an institution that is generally viewed as really freaking conservative, one that leftists have seen as a foe for decades, has to say:

The Israelites' experience of living as homeless aliens was so painful and frightening that God ordered his people for all time to have special care for the alien: "You shall treat the alien who resides with you no differently than the natives born among you; have the same love for him as for yourself; for you too were once aliens in the land of Egypt" (Lv 19:33–34)... First Principle: People have the right to migrate to sustain their lives and the lives of their families.

—United States Conference of Catholic Bishops, *Welcoming the Stranger Among Us: Unity in Diversity*

Well that's awkward. A 'right to migrate' is the very same thing that some of the more extreme atheist libertarians like to invoke. Perhaps a different church...

When a foreigner resides among you in your land, do not mistreat them. The foreigner residing among you must be treated as your native-born. Love them as yourself, for you were foreigners in Egypt. I am the Lord your God.—(Leviticus 19:33–34)... The arrival of migrants to the United States from so many parts of the world has also meant that there is a diversity of cultures and worldviews. The diversity of cultures, worldviews, and languages has placed an enormous strain upon migrants. To effectively deal with this trauma and ease the process of acculturation, migrants should be encouraged to preserve strong cultural and familial ties to their culture of origin.

—United Methodist Church, *Book of Resolutions*

What a curious coincidence that the Methodists quote a different translation of the same biblical verse. However instead of a right to migrate, they specifically call for immigrants to retain the culture of their homeland and refuse to assimilate to the culture of the place they've invaded. Under an open-borders regime, with millions of immigrants simultaneously arriving from different and possibly hostile cultures, that could prove interesting, as the Jews of France have recently learned. Of course, the Methodists are known as a fairly liberal denomination. So let's look at the Christians whom every leftist in America considers to be fire-breathing racists who would like nothing better than to re-institute slavery:

> *The motivations behind this generous spirit were that the people of God were not to forget that they had been strangers in Egypt (Exodus 22:21; Leviticus 19:33–34) Immigrant communities offer a new, vibrant field for evangelism, church planting, and ministry. Denominations have launched efforts to bring the gospel to these newcomers, establish churches, and train leaders for immigrant believers. Millions of immigrants also come from Christian backgrounds. These brothers and sisters in Christ are revitalizing churches across the country and are planting churches and evangelizing. Their presence is a blessing of God.*

> —National Association of Evangelicals, Resolution on Immigration, 2009

Ah, look, Leviticus 19:33–34 again, though merely paraphrased this time. 'Blessing of God' does seem a bit far from a stern anti-immigrant position however. It is beginning to look as if the entire mainstream Christian establishment of the United States is in rough agreement with the left in concluding that immigration is fantastic, multiculturalism is desirable, and open borders are a downright blessing to the nation.

Well then...

And so it seems that utopian leftists and libertarians, the most cynically realist business interests, and ever eager-to-please Cuckservatives are all in agreement that it would, on the whole, be better if you, Mr. American Worker, made less money and faced a lot more recently imported competition for your job. Also, you should be hip with the times and get used to those recent competitors voting to transfer a bunch of your money to themselves, seeing signs everywhere in their languages, and having to press '1' to get your own language in your own country. While we're at it, it would be best if you didn't make a fuss about people trekking across your property, or a few things going missing here and there. And if a few hundred extra million people show up to vote for a president-for-life, police and DMV clerks start demanding bribes to do their jobs, the country starts having regular power shortages, or the water is no longer always *quite* safe to drink, well hey... they tried.

While it's all going on, they, your betters, will be sitting behind security gates, laughing at you over drinks and snarking 'dere takin' our jerbs!' to each other in imitation redneck voices.

Oh, and also, you're a bigot and a racist if you have a problem with any of that.

Sound good to you?

There is literally no limit to the utter madness of the open-borders enthusiasts. That may sound like a strong statement, but as supporting evidence, we submit the words of Finland's Immigration Service Director, Esko Repo, concerning the case of one Ramin Azimi, an Afghan migrant who raped and murdered his 17-year-old Finnish girlfriend by burning her to death after she ended their month-long relationship. Mr. Repo declared that neither the rape nor the murder would be taken into account with regards to Mr. Azimi's application for political asylum and citizenship, saying that "while crimes committed abroad prior to arriving in Finland would be taken into account during the asylum decision process, ones perpetrated after arrival were not."

Chapter 7

Immigration and Economics

At an absolute minimum, economics should not be abused to "prove" the inappropriateness of caring about national economic well-being—something it does not do. From the point of view of pure economics, internationalist assumptions are as arbitrary as nationalist ones. People who reject the national economic interest should do so openly, not hide behind theoretical constructs that do this on the sly.

—Ian Fletcher, *Free Trade Doesn't Work: What Should Replace It and Why* (2010)

The blanket assertion that immigration is good for the economy has been the primary response of cuckservatives and other immigration proponents to critics of immigration for decades. The argument was used to push the 1965 Immigration and Nationality Act, it was used to justify the 1986 Immigration Amnesty, and it has been used to support everything from the failed Comprehensive Immigration Reform Acts of 2006 and 2007 that would have granted 12 million illegal aliens "a path to citizenship" to the Obama administration's 2014 executive action, which indefinitely deferred the deportation of 5 million illegal immigrants and granted them the right to work legally in the United States.

However, even if we set aside the philosophical question of whether the economic benefits of immigration automatically trump all the cultural, criminal, social, and opportunity costs, even if we elect to ignore the balance between economic growth and societal disruption, this still leaves one very important question that requires addressing: is immigration good for the economy?

It also implies a second, even more important question: is immigration good for Americans? Is it *economically beneficial* for American citizens? Cuckservative politicians certainly claim it is. In addition to his famously strange claim that that "illegal immigration is an act of love," open-borders enthusiast ¡Jeb! Bush also declared that "immigrants create an engine of economic prosperity" because "immigrants are more fertile." This would explain why, with an average crude birth rate 3.4 times that of the United States, Uganda, Mali, and Burkina Faso are the most economically prosperous societies in the world.

Unfortunately, ¡Jeb! is far from alone in his delusion. Immigration proponents have always been very quick to answer both questions in the affirmative without ever supplying any empirical justification for their claims because even the most basic classical economics theory casts an amount of serious doubt on the idea that immigration is intrinsically beneficial to a nation. After all, the Law of Supply and Demand indicates that an increase in supply when demand remains constant will lead to a decrease in price, so it is obvious that more immigrant labor means lower wages for American workers, even if it doesn't necessarily mean fewer jobs.

Moreover, the empirical evidence strongly supports the theory, as despite more than four decades of economic growth, at an inflation-corrected $3.72, real wages are eight percent below the average hourly wage of $4.03 in January 1973.

Were the Mongols an economic benefit to China? Did the Huns provide a significant boost to the economies of Eastern Europe? Did Vandal immigration restore or ravage the imperial Roman economy? Comparatively advanced as they were, English and Spanish immigrants nevertheless proved to be detriments to the primitive Native American tribal economies. The answer to the question of whether immigration is good for Americans is considerably more complicated than one usually hears from either the conservative or the mainstream media.

Due to these complications, an entire academic-media complex has developed over time, one devoted to explaining away the unavoidable observations concerning immigration's inevitable effect on the supply-demand curve for labor in the U.S. economy. This complex operates at various levels of sophistication, ranging from ignorant appeals to Adam Smith and David Ricardo to published papers utilizing sadistically complicated mathematics that require doctorates in Mathematics, Economics, and Advanced Daemonology to fully comprehend.

The idea that immigration always benefits the economy is intrinsically tied to the popular idea that free trade creates economic growth. Most individuals on the political right, from religious conservatives to anarcho-libertarians, harbor strong emotional attachments to free trade and capitalism, which they tend to consider essentially synonymous. And to be fair, there is a powerful rhetorical argument to be made for free trade that is bound to appeal to anyone who values liberty and human freedom.

Immigration and Free Trade

To understand this chapter, it is first necessary to understand that the arguments for immigration are the same as the arguments for free trade, because, technically speaking, immigration is a subset of free trade. While the most famous arguments for free trade have been made in terms of goods, they have nevertheless always necessarily included the free movement of capital, services, and labor as well. In fact, two of the Four Freedoms of the European Union refer implicitly to immigration by establishing the right of the free movement of workers as well as the freedom to provide services in addition to the two other components of free trade, goods and capital. The Four Freedoms are:

1. Free Movement of Goods

2. Freedom of Movement for Workers

3. Right of Establishment and Freedom to Provide Services

4. Free Movement of Capital

American conservatives have had a strong affinity for free trade for decades. Some of the most revered intellectual figures on the right have historically been among the most influential voices in favor of free trade. Milton Friedman's *Free To Choose* had a tremendous impact on millions of Republicans in the early 1980s. More esoteric, but highly influential economists such as Ludwig von Mises and Henry Hazlitt provided the foundation for intellectual arguments that were very nearly as convincing in their support of international free trade and the free movement of peoples as they were against goverment intervention in the domestic economy.

The logical extension of that foundation by the followers of Friedman, Mises, and Hazlitt was a sensible one and appealed greatly to every conservative with the sense to distrust the federal government. If the government could not be trusted to set prices or tell you with whom you could do business on a domestic basis, how did the invisible, arbitrary line that separated the domestic market from the international market magically grant the government the right, or the competence, to do so on an international basis? Both the politicians and the corporate executives who seldom otherwise agreed with the intellectual leaders of the right cheerfully embraced their reasoning on this point and rapidly went about dismantling every obstacle to the free movement of capital, goods, services, and people that might inhibit anyone, anywhere, from making a dollar on the basis of a mutually agreeable transaction.

The core foundation of this vast and growing global enthusiasm for economic freedom was David Ricardo's theory of comparative advantage. This was somewhat ironic, as his theory was predicated on the immobility of labor, but the free traders' pro-immigration argument, although never stated outright in a coherent logical manner, went something like this:

1. David Ricardo proved that free trade was to the benefit of both nations trading with the Theory of Comparative Advantage.

2. Free trade therefore promotes economic growth in a nation as measured in GDP.

3. GDP consists of goods and services.

4. Services are provided by people.

5. People who are situated outside the country have to be able to enter it at will in order to provide their services.

6. Therefore, allowing people to move freely across national borders will create economic growth.

This reasoning, as well as the fact that the United States, where people were able to move freely from one state to another, enjoyed faster rates of economic growth than the similarly advanced nations of Europe, where it was much more difficult to move from one nation to another, inspired the European nations to not only enshrine immigration into the Four Freedoms of the European Union, but to completely dismantle their borders with the 1985 Schengen Agreement that now covers 26 European nations, four of which are not actually E.U. member states.

The problem with what has become a quasi-religious belief in the beneficial nature of immigration and free trade is that David Ricardo never proved anything about the benefits of free trade in either goods or services. David Ricardo was not really an economist, he was a successful politician and gambler whose economic works were written as rhetorical polemics in an English political dispute over its Corn Laws. His work should not be read as a philosophical work of political economy, but as a political advertisement that merits no more serious contemplation than an automotive company's pamphlet explaining why the government should subsidize car exports or a pharmaceutical company's television ad for a newly developed drug.

Ricardo had a number of peculiar ideas, none of which are taken even a little bit seriously by economists today. In addition to the theory of comparative advantage, he also advocated the cost-of-production theory of value, which is a precursor of Karl Marx's long-outdated Labor Theory of Value, as well as the insane price-of-corn theory of profit. His method of presenting an argument was so hopelessly inept that Joseph Schumpeter openly mocked it in his epic *History of Economic Analysis*.

> *His interest was in the clear-cut result of direct, practical significance. In order to get this he cut that general system to pieces, bundled up as large parts of it as possible, and put them in cold storage—so that as many things as possible should be frozen and 'given'. He then piled one simplifying assumption upon another until, having really settled everything by these*

assumptions, he was left with only a few aggregative variables between which, given these assumptions, he set up simple one-way relations so that, in the end, the desired results emerged almost as tautologies.... The habit of applying results of this character to the solution of practical problems we shall call the Ricardian Vice.

Furthermore, David Ricardo did not even originate the theory with which his name is synonymous, but instead borrowed the concept from Robert Torrens, who introduced the theory of comparative advantage in *An Essay on the External Corn Trade.*

But let us not do as SJWs and cuckservatives do, and pretend that simply disqualifying Ricardo suffices to settle the question of whether immigration is good for the economy or not. The more substantive objection is that the model Ricardo constructed to make his case is set in a world where goods and capital are mobile, but labor remains fixed. He described a scenario where two countries, Britain and Portugal, both produce cloth and wine, but at different levels of efficiency. Portugal produces cloth 10 percent less expensively than Britain, and produces wine at a 27 percent discount.

Table 7.1: Unit Labor Costs

Britain	100 cloth	110 wine
Portugal	90 cloth	80 wine

According to Ricardo, in the absence of transportation costs, it is most efficient for Britain to produce only cloth, and Portugal to produce only wine, since, assuming that the two goods trade at an equal price (one unit of cloth for one unit of wine), Britain can then obtain wine at a cost of 100 labor units by producing cloth and trading it, rather than spend 110 units to produce the wine itself, and Portugal can obtain cloth at a cost of 80 units by trade rather than 90 by production.

Therefore, Ricardo's conclusion is that even though Britain could produce both its own cloth and wine, it is to Britain's benefit to specialize in producing only cloth, selling it, and buying imported Portuguese wine with the proceeds. It is this argument that is known as the theory of comparative advantage, and on the basis of little more than Ricardo's imaginary model, economists have concluded that free trade necessarily benefits all national economies and every political institution from NAFTA to the European Union that claims to be dedicated to free trade is therefore justified.

However, this hypothetical and outdated world where capital and goods are mobile and labor is immobile is not actually relevant to the world we presently inhabit, so let us consider the theory of comparative advantage in a mobile-labor scenario that utilizes Ricardo's original postulates from *On the Principles of Political Economy and Taxation*. To do so, we introduce immigration into the equation through the free movement of labor. Now that labor is permitted to move as easily as goods, *both* wine and cloth laborers will move to Britain, since they believe they will receive an 11 percent raise and a 38 percent raise respectively. However, once they get there, the doubling of the labor supply in Britain this immigration causes will quickly cause the price of labor to fall, and it will fall considerably.

From the economic perspective, this is fantastic for Britain! It can now produce the same amount of cloth as before for price of only 47.5 units of labor, and the same amount of wine for 47.5 labor units as well. Britain will thereby produce an equal quantity of both wine and cloth *for less than what it used to cost* to produce the wine alone. This increase in production will vastly increase profits in the British cloth and wine industries, as well as creating a windfall for the financial industry investing in those industries!

As you can see here, what the economists completely fail to consider is whether what is good for the owners of the British cloth and wine industries, and their bankers, is actually good for anyone else in Britain.

Those massive new profits exist because wages have fallen by 50 percent, and since the costs of other goods haven't fallen in line with the reduced wages of the British workers who still have their jobs, their quality of life declines. Other consequences include how the newly unemployed British workers may go on the dole or turn to crime, how the new Portuguese immigrants are heavily inclined to vote for the Labour Party (thereby throwing the British political system out of balance), and how British women begin bearing half-Portuguese children, thereby lowering the average IQ of the next generation by two IQ points or more, but in the short term, these factors are all considered "non-economic" and therefore don't count as far as the economists are concerned.

They sound suspiciously familiar, though, don't they?

In conclusion, this neo-Ricardian model "proves" open immigration and the free movement of labor is not only economically desirable, but is vastly preferable to the immobile-labor comparative advantage model by a factor of 105/200 and to autarky by a factor of 105/210. Immigration is always good for every economy!

What else can we conclude from this unseemly exercise of the Ricardian Vice?

- Ricardo implicitly postulated the immobility of labor.

- The mobility of labor not only fails to disprove comparative advantage, but actually strengthens the case for even freer trade...

at least if you're in the higher-labor-cost country and you only look at the labor costs.

- The mobility of labor will eliminate international trade since everyone will be living in Britain.

- The mobility of labor operates to the extreme detriment of labor and wage rates.

- Ricardo's logic is irrelevant, proves absolutely nothing, and does not provide a credible basis for defending either free trade or immigration.

But these are abstract and theoretical arguments, and while the theoretical approach might have made sense in 1965, when there was little economic data to be had, or even in 1986, when the contrast between the stagflation of the 1970s and the Reagan boom of the 1980s is believed by economists to have had considerably more to do with lower tax and interest rates than immigration, this is no longer the case in 2015. Considering that we now have fifty years of immigration and economic data to analyze, a more empirical approach is not only possible, but is capable of clearly determining once and for all whether immigration of the nature and scale observed over the last five decades has been good for the economy or not.

Immigration, Jobs, and the U.S. Economy

If immigration is good for the economy, then a comparison of the annual growth of the U.S. Gross Domestic Product (GDP) with annual immigration rates should show a strong and consistent positive correlation. If it does not, that does not mean that we can conclude immigration is bad for the economy, only that the pro-immigration arguments that claim immigration is good for the economy are false. Of course, if we find a strong and consistent negative correlation between GDP growth and immigration, that will permit us to point out that immigration *is* actually bad for the economy.

But the economy is an abstract concept, which is why we need to look at the question of whether immigration is actually good for Americans or not. Of what use is a growing economy that doesn't materially benefit the people living in that society? To determine whether immigration is materially beneficial for Americans or not, we must look at three factors:

1. the real median household income

2. the number of jobs available

3. the average wages paid by those jobs

As with the growth of the national economy, if five decades of immigration has resulted in more jobs paying higher wages, which will necessarily translate into higher median household income, we will have to conclude that immigration is economically beneficial to Americans. And if it has not, it will be readily apparent that Americans have been sold a false bill of goods by cuckservatives and other immigration proponents.

In the 50 years since the 1965 Immigration Reform Act opened the floodgates, 59 million immigrants have arrived in the United States. Combined with their children and grandchildren, these immigrants have accounted for more than half the nation's population growth. Are they also responsible for most of the economic growth of the last five decades as well?

There is absolutely no statistical indication that this is the case. Since 1967, annual U.S. economic growth, measured in GDP, has averaged 2.8 percent, ranging from a peak of 7.3 percent in 1984 to a low of -2.8 percent in 2009. During that same period, annual immigration growth averaged 4.5 percent, but with considerably more variance, as post-1965 immigration growth peaked in 1989 at 70.0 percent and hit a bottom at -46.7 percent in 1992.

In statistics, the correlation coefficient r compares the strength and direction of a linear relationship between two variables. The value of r is always between +1 and -1, with +1 indicating a perfect correlation and -1 indicating a perfectly negative correlation. For U.S. economic growth and immigration growth from 1967 through 2013, r is equal to 0.04, which is below the 0.3 level that indicates a weak correlation and is essentially equal to no correlation at all. So, while we can't conclude on this basis that immigration is bad for the economy, we can state that there is no statistical evidence that it is good for the economy either.

To determine whether immigration is good for Americans, we will look at median household income, which refers to the household income that is in the precise middle of all American households and is corrected for inflation. As before, if there is a strong positive correlation between median household income and immigration, then we can conclude that immigration is good for American families, and if there is a negative correlation, we can conclude that it is bad for them.

From 1967 to 2013, the most recent year for which the information is available, real median household income in the United States rose from \$42,934 to \$52,250. The best year for American families was 1972, when it rose by \$1,955. The worst year was 2008, when it fell by -\$1,983. Over that 47-year period, r is equal to -0.33, which indicates a weak negative correlation between immigration and real median household income. This indicates that immigration tends to be bad for American families.

Now to the question of jobs and whether immigration tends to create more of them or whether immigrants tend to take American jobs and reduce American wages. Early in the 2016 election cycle, the media attacked both Democratic and Republican presidential candidates for daring to suggest that immigration is the reason for persistent American unemployment.

> *Sanders' position on immigration has been called "complicated" and he has been criticized by immigration activists for supporting the idea that immigrants coming to the U.S. are taking jobs and hurting the economy, a theory that has been proven incorrect. Both of his leading Democratic challengers, Hillary Clinton and Martin O'Malley, have recognized that new immigrants coming to the country actually boost the economy. But Sanders continues to align himself more closely with Democratic positions of the past.*

> *"I frankly do not believe that we should be bringing in significant numbers of unskilled to workers to compete with [unemployed] kids," Sanders said. "I want to see these kids get jobs."*

> *Studies have shown that immigrants actually create jobs for American workers. Researchers recently found that each new immigrant has produced about 1.2 new jobs in the U.S., most of which have gone to native-born workers. And according to the Atlantic, an influx in immigration can cause non-tradable professions—jobs like hospitality and construction that cannot be outsourced—to see a wage increase because the demand for goods and services grows with the expanding population.*

> —"Why Immigration Is The Hole In Bernie Sanders' Progressive Agenda", *ThinkProgress*, 30 July 2015

The ThinkProgress claims were based on the National Bureau of Economic Research Working Paper No. 21123, entitled "Are Immigrants a Shot in the Arm for the Local Economy?" issued in April 2015 by Gihoon Hong and John McLaren. Based on U.S. Census data from 1980 to 2000, it studied the effects of local labor demand and purported to provide evidence that proved the additional demand for labor created by immigration more than made up for the additional supply provided by the additional workers. Some of the claims from the paper were as follows:

- Each immigrant creates 1.2 local jobs for local workers, most of them going to native workers, and 62 percent of these jobs are in non-traded services.

- Consistent with our prediction, the impacts of immigration on employment growth have become greater as the estimates imply that each new immigrant is predicted to add 2.5 new jobs (1.9 for native workers) to a city in which he or she settles.

There are two significant problems with the evidence provided by the authors, as both the time period and the area scope are cherry-picked to provide data that supports the conclusion the authors wanted to reach. The first problem is that the 20 years between 1980 and 2000 were the height of the credit boom during which the U.S. economy nearly doubled in size, growing from $6.5 trillion in 1980 to $12.7 trillion in 2000 according to the Bureau of Economic Analysis. This left out the 2001 recession as well as the post-2008 depression, both of which had an observably negative effect on the number of U.S. jobs available. The 1980–2000 period also featured less immigration than the subsequent 15 years, as the Department of Homeland security reported an average of 841,149 annual immigrants, 23 percent fewer than the 1,090,520 who arrived in each of the subsequent 15 years.

The second problem is that the data omits most of the country, most of the immigrants, and most of the jobs by focusing on 219 METAREAS, or metropolitan areas that included 7,026,535 workers, of whom 1,053,980 were immigrants. This compares to the actual national figures of 115.2 million jobs and 42.6 million immigrants in the United States in the year 2000. If the data that represented six percent of the jobs and 2.5 percent of the immigrants had been statistically sampled, it might be relevant. But since it was cherry-picked in a manner that logic would suggest is likely to minimize the effects of immigration on American jobs, it cannot be.

This cherry-picking is inexcusable in light of the fact that the Bureau of Labor Statistics makes the national employment data readily available on a monthly basis so there is no need to study local labor effects and then extrapolate them to the national level, we can simply look at the national effects. There are a number of different statistics that can be used, but for the sake of simplicity and avoiding estimates we will use four basic statistics:

- The U.S. working-age population (15–64) published by the Federal Reserve Bank of St. Louis.

- The Civilian Employment-Population Ratio published by the Bureau of Labor Statistics that tracks the percentage of the working-age (16 years or older) population that is employed.

- The number of legal immigrants arriving annually in the United States published by the Department of Homeland Security. This includes refugees.

- The number of illegal immigrants estimated to be resident in the United States, published by the Pew Research Center.

In 1980, the U.S. working age population was 142,520,008 and the employment-population ratio was 60.0. That means there were 85,512,005 jobs in 1980. In the 35 years from 1980 to 2015, 33,180,780 legal immigrants and 11.3 million illegal immigrants arrived for a total of 44,480,780 immigrants. If each immigrant created sufficient demand to create 2.5 new jobs, that would mean that there would have to be at least 196,713,955 jobs in the United States in 2015.

The U.S. working age population in 2015 was 204,026,416, which is in line with the 44.5 million immigrants. However, the employment-population ratio dropped to 59.3, meaning that there were only 120,987,665 jobs in the United States, or 75,726,290 less than expected. Each immigrant did not create 2.5 new jobs, or even 1.2 new jobs; even if we assume that every single new job created in the United States between 1980 and 2015 was the direct result of immigration and not entrepreneurial activity or technological progress, the maximum number of jobs that could possibly have been created is 0.8 per immigrant.

That means that every working immigrant costs American workers at least one-fifth of a job. And there is additional statistical evidence to support this conclusion, as the employment-population ratio for native-born workers has fallen since the Bureau of Labor Statistics began tracking it, from 62.7 percent in 2007 to 59 percent in 2015. It also explains why real median household income negatively correlates with immigration, since American workers are working fewer jobs at lower wages than they would be in the absence of immigration.

It is therefore apparent that the pro-immigration economic models are incorrect and the empirical evidence is in line with the economic theory. Immigration is bad for the economy because immigrant workers do, in fact, take jobs away from American workers.

Immigration and the Free Movement of International Labor

Free trade advocates often claim that there is no reason for any difference between the U.S. domestic economy and the international economy. They believe there should be no more barriers between sovereign nation-states than there are between the several and united American States. And yet, look at the difference between labor mobility in the USA versus the European Union.

In the former EU15, only about 0.1 percent of the working age population changes its country of residence in a given year. Conversely, in the U.S., about three percent of the working age population moves to a different state every year.

> *These institutional and cultural differences suggest comparing internal geographical mobility in the U.S. with the situation within EU member states rather than between member states. In doing so, the figures narrow the mobility gap between Europe and the United States. Between 2000 and 2005, about one percent of the working age population had changed residence each year from one region to another within the EU15 countries, compared to an overall interstate mobility rate of 2.8 to 3.4 percent in the U.S. during the same period of time.*

—Peter Ester and Hubert Krieger, "Comparing labour mobility in Europe and the US: facts and pitfalls", 2008

What this means is that U.S. workers are about three times more willing to change their state of residence than European workers are willing to change their region of residence within national borders, and 30x more inclined to change their state of residence than Europeans are inclined to change their country of residence, even though the U.S. state-to-state change likely involves a bigger geographic move than the EU country-to-country one.

It should be noted that not only is increasing this country-to-country labor mobility rate within the EU a major goal of the EU's economic advisers, but the explicitly stated reason for this goal is their belief that increased labor mobility is required in order to increase economic growth.

Now, let's look at what that annual three percent intra-U.S. mobility translates to in terms of the overall population. The statistics below represent the percentage of Americans between the ages of 25 and 44 who are still resident in their State of birth; a higher number represents a lower rate of intra-U.S. mobility:

- U.S.A.: 50.5 percent

- East: 54.3 percent

- Midwest: 65.0 percent

- South: 47.3 percent

- West: 40.2 percent

A lower mobility rate is why the Midwest has changed much less over the last 40 years than either the East Coast or the West Coast. More Midwesterners stay in the Midwest and maintain their laws and cultural traditions over time. But more importantly, note what this signifies for the USA if the apostles of free trade were ever able to achieve their goal of permitting international trade to take place on the same terms as American domestic trade in a manner that realized the expected economic benefits: very nearly half of all American workers would be expected to leave the USA by the average age of 35!

This vast exodus of young Americans would say nothing, of course, of the hundreds of millions of non-American workers who would be expected to enter the USA, with all of the various consequences to be expected as a result of immigration that is an order of magnitude larger than the current wave.

The logic of free trade and immigration is inescapable. It amounts to a choice between a steadily declining living standard if free trade is limited to goods and capital and the total destruction of the nation and the replacement of a majority of its population within a single lifetime if it is pursued to the full extent of the concept.

The Vox Day Argument Against Free Trade

But our argument against free trade, the free movement of labor, and immigration does not rest on David Ricardo's intellectual corpse or empirical data from the Bureau of Economic Analysis. It is not even, strictly speaking, economic in nature. This is the basic four-step Vox Day Argument Against Free Trade.

- Free trade, in its true, complete, and intellectually coherent form, is not limited to the free movement of goods, but includes the free movement of capital and labor as well. The "invisible judicial line" doesn't magically become visible simply because human bodies are involved instead of goods or capital.

- The difference between domestic economies and the global international economy is not trivial, but is substantive, material, and based on significant genetic, cultural, traditional, and legal differences between various self-identified peoples.

- Free trade is totally incompatible with national sovereignty, democracy, and self-determination, as well as the existence of independent nation-states with the right and ability to set their own laws according to the preferences of their nationals.

- Therefore, free trade must be opposed by every sovereign, democratic, or self-determined people, be they American, Chinese, German, or Zambian, who wish to preserve themselves as a free and distinct nation possessed of its own culture, traditions, and laws.

In light of the massive quantity of evidence, both theoretical and empirical, against the beneficial nature of immigration, this naturally raises the question if a pro-immigration, pro-free-trade stance can reasonably be considered conservative. There is, after all, nothing conservative about importing tens of millions of people from different cultures and political traditions. Moreover, we are assured, from the most impeccable of reliable left-wing sources, that free trade is an inherently anti-conservative concept that "hastens the social revolution."

> *If the free-traders cannot understand how one nation can grow rich at the expense of another, we need not wonder, since these same gentlemen also refuse to understand how within one country one class can enrich itself at the expense of another.... But, in general, the protective system of our day is conservative, while the free trade system is destructive. It breaks up old nationalities and pushes the antagonism of the proletariat and the bourgeoisie to the extreme point. In a word, the free trade system hastens the social revolution. It is in this revolutionary sense alone, gentlemen, that I vote in favor of free trade.*
>
> —*On the Question of Free Trade*, Karl Marx, 1848

There is nothing less conservative than supporting social revolution. And there is nothing more cuckservative than embracing a radical left-wing ideology that favors foreign workers over American workers, and supporting economic policies that *absolutely ensure* one's children will be forced out of the nest of their own country before they are 35. Indeed, the greatest crime of the cuckservatives has been the way in which they have made it possible for 59 million aliens to invade America to the detriment of American families and American society, while resisting every rational attempt by genuine conservatives and patriotic Americans to defend their country, their family interests, and their way of life.

Chapter 8

Immigration and War

Where today are the Pequot? Where are the Narragansett, the Mohican, the Pokanoket, and many other once powerful tribes of our people? They have vanished before the avarice and the oppression of the White Man, as snow before a summer sun. Will we let ourselves be destroyed in our turn without a struggle, give up our homes, our country bequeathed to us by the Great Spirit, the graves of our dead and everything that is dear to us?

—Tecumseh, Chief of the Shawnee, speech before the
Choctaw and Chickasaw nations, 1811

Tecumseh was the Shawnee chief who led the last great coalition of the eastern Indian tribes in alliance with Great Britain against the United States during the War of 1812. Widely regarded in his own time as a powerful and eloquent speaker, Tecumseh was also among the first known Native American leaders to see the struggle with white settlers as something larger than a matter of individual tribal politics.

But no doubt, he was just a xenophobe and racist, right? After all, everything turned out fine for the Shawnee, Choctaw, Chickasaw,

Cherokee and the other tribes, as in the end they were able to peacefully assimilate the European immigrants into their societies.

Right?

Many SJWs and leftists are quite willing to condemn the historical behavior of the English and Spanish colonists towards the American Indian. They will readily concur that this one particular example of mass immigration turned out poorly for the native-born inhabitants. But they resolutely refuse to admit that this is true of mass immigration in general. Instead, they insist that the mass migration to the Americas by Europeans was nothing more than an example of the unique evil of racist, Christian, cis-gendered white people. Or something. And since this negative outcome for the natives was unique, they insist that any other form of mass immigration, today or in the past, could not possibly have anything in common with it.

And it isn't just the left who implicitly views immigration through a template of American exceptionalism. Today, almost everyone recognizes that the Native Americans were subjected to harsh and often treacherous treatment, though few understand how or why it happened. Today's cuckservatives also feel their own measure of white guilt over the plight of the American Indian, although most of their sympathy is reserved for blacks. Yet virtually no conservative dares to make the obvious comparison between the earlier waves of European migration to the Americas and the mass migration of other peoples and other cultures into the United States and Europe today. But the comparison is not only legitimate, it is *necessary*. When considering the probable effects of the current migrations, it should not be forgotten that mass migration, followed by inter-ethnic war, defeated, drove out, and suppressed the original inhabitants of North America in favor of the invading newcomers.

Modern readers tend to see these two phenomena—immigration and war—as being entirely different. War is seen as the realm of organized armies of recognizable soldiers (or at the very least, tribal warriors), whereas immigration is seen as the movement of peaceful families. Yet most of the fighting on the American frontiers, between the European immigrants and the native inhabitants, did not take place between organized, national armies. Nor was open war and military force the only means by which the American Indians were driven off their land. Mass immigration did most of the work by itself, as through the arrival and settlement of newcomers with drastically different ways of life, in large enough numbers and with sufficient cultural self-confidence to feel no need to assimilate to the native population.

The fact of the matter is that for all intents and purposes, large-scale immigration *is* war.

History bears this out. Consider just a few, a very few, of the historical examples of immigration leading directly to war. The particular names and dates involved are less important here than the common patterns that they represent. For the fact is, the challenges presently faced by the United States and other Western nations today with regards to mass immigration are neither new nor unique.

The Sea Peoples

In the 13th century BC, the Bronze Age empires in Egypt and the Near East came under ultimately fatal pressure from new migrating populations, not organized armies or empires, but entire migrating peoples with women and children. They swiftly grew in numbers and violence, escalating into the largest immigration crisis in history up to that point.

These newcomers were largely from the northern shores of the Mediterranean, including northern Greece, Sardinia, Sicily, and western Anatolia. They may have included the ancestors of the Etruscans and the Philistines. They were seafarers, and in modern times have been collectively termed 'The Sea Peoples'. While they came with their families, they still came with war. One early description of them from Egyptian sources is reminiscent of descriptions of the Vikings from centuries later:

> *The unruly Sherden whom no one had ever known how to combat, they came boldly sailing in their warships from the midst of the sea, none being able to withstand them.*

At the time of their first appearance, Egypt was at the height of its power under pharaoh Ramses II. He sent soldiers against the newcomers, killing some, and incorporated others into his army as mercenaries. Later pharaohs tried various policies with less successful results. Eventually, in the 12th century BC, Ramses III expelled them from his lands, forcibly resettled some of them in Canaan, and raised a large fleet to keep them at bay.

Other nations also tried to either absorb or co-opt the newcomers; some even tried taking them into their service as soldiers. They were less successful than the Egyptians. A large number of Sea People settled in Libya, overwhelmed the indigenous kings there, and from there attacked Egypt by land. The Hittite empire, the Mittani kingdom, and the Mycenaean civilization of Crete all collapsed at the time of the mass migrations. The majority of sizable cities in southern Greece, Crete, Cyprus, eastern Anatolia, and the eastern coast of the Mediterranean show an archaeological layer of destruction from this time period. Some were never rebuilt.

An entirely separate group of invaders—Semitic tribes from the deserts—took advantage of the chaotic situation and began a series of migratory invasions of their own. Eventually, Egypt too collapsed into disorder. Notably, of all the great Bronze Age nations, only the militaristic and comparatively xenophobic Assyrian Empire survived intact. A surviving Egyptian inscription is observably similar to the apocalyptic tone of Tecumseh's speech to his fellow American Indians:

> *The foreign countries made a conspiracy in their islands, All at once the lands were removed and scattered in the fray. No land could stand before their arms: from Hatti, Qode, Carchemish, Arzawa and Alashiya on, being destroyed at one time. A camp was set up in Amurru. They desolated its people, and its land was like that which has never come into being.*

Carthage and the Sicilian Wars

There is some archeological evidence a group of Sea People settled on the eastern coast of the Mediterranean and became the people known in the Bible as Philistines. Their neighbors to the north were an ancient seagoing people known as the Phoenicians, whose three great cities were Byblos, Tyre, and Sidon. A maritime power and trading empire, they set up trading settlements all along the coasts, the most important of which was the "New City" established by emigrants from Tyre in 814 BC on the northern coast of Africa. When King Cyrus the Great of Persia conquered Phoenicia in 539 BC and divided it into four vassal kingdoms, followed by Alexander the Great taking Tyre by siege in 332 BC, Carthage became the leading city of the Phoenician world.

Enriched by its colonies in Spain, where vast quantities of silver were mined, Carthage grew into an even larger, more powerful Mediterranean empire that stretched from Spain to Numidia and ruled over more than 300 cities. The Carthaginians also established colonies of their own, including several on the rich agricultural island of Sicily, where they, along with the Iberian Sicans, the Italian Sicels, and the native Elymians all lived in reasonably balanced politico-economic synergy.

However, the Greeks also set up colonies there, one of which became the wealthy and powerful city of Syracuse, and their colonial modus operandi is described as usually involving "the violent expulsion of indigenous communities." Over time, the rivalry between the Greeks and the Carthaginians intensified, culminating in a series of four sieges of Syracuse between 397 and 278 BC. While all four of the sieges ultimately failed, other cities on the island were taken by the invading Carthaginians and some were sacked, including Messina, where the entire population was driven out; entire armies were destroyed; and plague struck both Northern Africa and Sicily.

The native people, caught up in the middle of the wars between the two sets of immigrants, suffered the worst. As historian Richard Miles described it:

> Through the enslaving of the defeated, the capturing of cities, and war reparations, conflict provided the funds to preserve the bloody status quo between Carthage and Syracuse on the island. The real victims were the Punic, indigenous, and Sicilian Greek cities in whose name this bloody process was perpetuated. Such was the brutal economy of war.

But it was war that would not have occurred in the first place were it not for the preceding waves of immigration.

Rome and the Germanic Migrations

Near the end of the second century AD, the Roman Empire stood at the height of its power. The Roman economy reached levels of size and sophistication that would not be seen for another thousand years or more, and civil engineering, including fresh water and sanitation, not until the 19th century. Estimates of literacy among the population range as high as 30 percent—which however low by modern standards, was higher than any other society of the time, and higher than would be seen again until the Renaissance. Rome had the first professional military organized along lines that would be recognizable to modern soldiers.

Although the emperors themselves, autocratic dictators along the lines of Latin American *caudillos*, had ruled for two centuries, they operated within a vast framework of government established during the Roman republic. Life for most inhabitants of the empire was lived under regular codified laws that in turn formed the basis of European legal systems to the present day. Yet two centuries later, it was all crumbling. A century after that, the Roman state and civilization in the west had been swept away entirely. What happened?

The fall of the Roman Empire is a subject that has been debated by historians for centuries, and it would be well beyond the scope of this book to attempt to provide some sort of comprehensive answer here. But what all of them have agreed upon is the critical role played by mass immigration—in this case the migration of the Germanic peoples—in that fall.

Parallels between Roman and American history have been made by many other writers, but one that is of interest here is the way in which the Romans expanded their influence by extending their citizenship to ever-widening groups of people. From, originally, only the inhabitants of the actual city of Rome and its outlying rural areas, it eventually came to encompass all the free inhabitants of the empire. There are modern writers who have seen the Roman Empire as a kind of melting pot, or a multicultural ideal, and in fact, there were even some in Roman times who did the same.

Consider the following excerpts from a speech by the Greek scholar Aelius Aristides, delivered in 155 AD in Rome itself:

> *Neither the sea nor the great expanse of intervening land keeps one from being a citizen, and there is no distinction between Europe and Asia.... in every city throughout the empire there are many who share citizenship with you, no less than they share citizenship with their fellow natives. And some of these Roman citizens have not even seen this city... You, better than anyone else, have proved the truth of the proverb: The earth is everyone's mother and our common fatherland.*

Writing nearly three centuries later, the poet Rutilius Namatianus echoed this view from Gaul:

> *For nations far apart you have made a single fatherland; under your dominion captivity has meant profit even for those who knew not justice, and by offering to the vanquished a share in your own justice, you have made a city of what was erstwhile a world.*

These writings parallel a confidence among the Roman leaders themselves that they could integrate foreigners into the Roman system. However, this expansion and integration of citizenship, and concurrent evolution in the values of those who held that citizenship, led to two distinct breakpoints in Roman history. The first, much earlier, was the breakdown of the republic and its replacement by the rule of emperors; the second, which concerns us here, was the ultimate failure of integration and the disintegration of the Empire itself in Western Europe.

Barbarian raids and wars had been recurring features along the Roman frontiers from the time they first stabilized. Beginning in the mid-4th century AD, a new phenomenon emerged—the arrival of entire

Germanic tribes, with men, women and children, seeking to migrate into Roman territory. The following story should sound familiar to readers who've observed the history of the Syrian refugee crisis.

In 376 AD, the homeland of the Goths, an eastern Germanic people, was torn by chaotic warfare, particularly against the invading Huns. Large numbers of Gothic tribespeople arrived at the Roman frontier on the Danube River, and asked for permission to enter the empire as refugees. At that time, the empire had two co-emperors, and the eastern emperor Valens agreed. He hoped to settle the newcomers as farmers and allied soldiers, *foederati*, under the traditional Roman system.

However, the Romans were completely unprepared for the scale of the Gothic immigration. The Goths, for their part, were not easily converted from their previous lives to that of peaceful peasant farmers. They were assembled in what were intended to be temporary camps, where conditions rapidly deteriorated. Within months, the refugees rioted and rose up in armed revolt. Valens attempted to deal with it as a kind of police action, which only succeeded in dragging things out for two years as the Goths engaged in a mobile campaign of looting and destruction throughout the Balkans.

At last, the deteriorating situation forced Valens to act. He called upon his western colleague, the emperor Gratian, for help, with the plan that they would crush the invaders with the overwhelming strength of their combined armies. Gratian agreed, and led an army from Gaul to assist, but was then delayed dealing with a migratory invasion of his own, by tribes of the western German Alamanni across the Rhine. Valens decided to press the war against the Goths by himself, and was instead defeated and killed by them at the battle of Adrianople.

Though his successors were eventually able to rebuild the army, they did so partly by recruiting barbarians themselves into its ranks. They never successfully expelled the newcomers, and those newcomers never fully integrated into Roman society. The long-term result was a permanent Gothic presence inside the borders of the empire, sometimes as wandering plunderers, sometimes as relatively loyal soldiers. After Adrianople, other Germanic groups began to enter the Empire, sometimes peacefully and sometimes not. In response, the imperial government made larger, and increasingly less successful, efforts to accommodate them.

The new and unpleasant reality of immigration and war in the empire itself led Gallic-Roman writer Sulpicius Severus to offer his own opinion on the Roman melting pot, one very different from the romantic American version:

> *Finally, by the mixture of pottery and iron, materials which never form a cohesive bond, which one after another are going to separate from each other, are signified in as much as it is well known that Roman soil has been occupied by foreign or rebellious peoples, or has been surrendered to those who have surrendered themselves through the fiction of peace, and we see barbarian peoples… which have been mixed into our armies, cities and provinces, living among us but not assimilating our customs.*

Things grew far more serious a generation after Adrianople, in 406 AD, when the still-ongoing warfare in Germany, along with a bitterly harsh winter, led a vast coalition of tribes to cross the Rhine. The border, heavily guarded for centuries, had four years earlier been stripped of much of its garrison by the general Stilicho—himself of Gothic origins. The migrants easily crossed the relatively undefended frontier, and proceeded to wander, taking what they wished and burning cities as they went. Again, remember, these were not armies, and not even raiding parties of warriors along the lines of the Vikings; these were entire populations with women and children in tow.

The results were catastrophic. Having failed to defend their borders, the Roman leadership found itself fighting, and slowly losing, running wars within the empire itself. Only four years later, the Visigoths, a branch of the Gothic refugees mentioned above, and nominally Roman allies, took advantage of the situation to plunder the city of Rome itself.

In the midst of the migration and destruction, there were those who, just like today, hoped the newcomers could be integrated into native society. In 417 AD, the Hispano-Roman Christian author Orosius wrote optimistically of conditions in Iberia at the time:

> *The barbarians, having forsworn their swords, have turned*
> *to the plow and nurture the surviving Romans as allies now,*
> *and friends.*

It must have been a comforting thought. There are revisionist, often multiculturalist, historians today who have created an entire school of theory dedicated to downplaying the havoc caused by the barbarian invasions. Yet the simple fact remains—at the beginning of the 5th century, there was a Roman Empire in Western Europe, and at the end there was not. Many inhabitants of the Empire were all too aware of what was happening:

> *The ancient Romans were feared, we are afraid. The barbar-*
> *ian peoples used to pay them tribute, we are dependent on*
> *the barbarians… How unfortunate we are! How far we have*
> *declined.*

> —Salvian of Marseilles,
> *On the Government of God*, c.440 AD

And remember, again, this was not a simple military invasion, merely replacing one set of rulers with another. The Germanic migrations involved widespread destruction, seizure of lands, and the partial replacement of the original inhabitants by the immigrant invaders, just as happened to many of the people of the Bronze-Age civilizations fifteen hundred years earlier, and as happened to the Native Americans a thousand years later. Consider the following words of despair written in 475 AD:

> *No longer will our ancestors even glory in this appellation, because they now begin to lose their descendants.*
>
> —Saint Sidonius Apollinaris, Bishop of Auvergne

The Arab Emigrations

One of the great misconceptions underlying almost all modern discussion of the Middle East is the idea that Arabs constitute some sort of indigenous people, as if they were the Old World equivalent of Native Americans. The reality is very different. From Morocco to Iraq, the pre-Islamic population consisted mostly of other non-Arab peoples, with very different cultural heritages, and the Arabs themselves were limited to the Arabian Peninsula. For example, the Carthaginian Empire of Phoenician descent described above was located in the modern Islamic states of Tunisia and Algeria. But the long process of immigration, conflict, violence, and state-backed cultural assimilation—to the culture of the immigrants, not the natives—began with the early expansion of Islam under the successors of Muhammad.

In 632 AD, Muhammad, the founder and prophet of Islam, died in Mecca, having consolidated his rule over a new empire that encompassed most of the peninsula. Near his death, he called for Islam to be spread over the entire world. His first successors, the caliphs, presided over an unruly collection of Arabic-speaking tribes, newly converted from paganism, who were readily capable of acting without central authority. On three sides they faced the sea, while to the north were the borders of the Persian and the Eastern Roman empires. The latter was by this time led by a Greek ruling class that successfully maintained its cultural cohesion, and therefore its existence, in contrast to the Latin-speaking Romans in the Western Empire.

Fortunately for the Arabs, the two great empires had exhausted themselves in a cataclysmic war some ten years earlier. While the armies of the caliphate defeated both empires in several conventional battles, the real work of conquest and consolidation was done by unorganized Arab tribes who poured across the poorly-defended frontiers, demanding conversion or submission as they went. For both *ghazis*, or Islamic warriors, and Bedouins, who travelled with their families and livestock, the Islamic religion and Arabic culture were one and the same. More often than not, they acted without any central coordination or authority, yet over time they replaced the indigenous cultures of the Middle East, and to some extent the populations as well, with their own.

One theme that emerged time and again during the Arabic conquests of this period was the disunity and indecision of the defending leadership. In both the Persian and the Byzantine empires, proto-cuckservatives appeared, local factions who preferred to appease and accommodate the invaders rather than fight them. In Egypt, de facto leadership fell to the Patriarch of Alexandria, who repeatedly undermined his own side's efforts to fight before signing a treaty of surrender in defiance of the Imperial government itself. In terms that will sound familiar to those who've followed the self-destructive travails of the Republican Party, the patriarch and his followers rationalized that the battles they faced were unwinnable, and therefore they should surrender and retreat—after which they would supposedly regroup in order to fight on more advantageous terms.

It didn't work out that way.

In Egypt, the majority of the overwhelmingly Christian population once spoke Coptic, a language descended from the ancient Egyptian of the Pharaohs, while a sizable minority spoke Greek. Today the population is overwhelmingly both Muslim and Arabic. In what is now Jordan, Syria, and Lebanon, the most common language was Aramaic, derived from that of the conquerors who had joined in the destruction of the Bronze-age civilizations two thousand years earlier. Now, the Aramaic-speaking peoples found themselves on the receiving end of the same process. In North Africa, the native population was largely Berber, Roman, and Punic. Today, there are only a handful of Aramaic speakers left in the world, the Punic language and culture have vanished entirely, and Berbers are a small and despised minority in their ancestral homelands.

The European populations of Iberia, Sicily, the Balkans, the Greek Islands, and even France would have met the same fate, had they not ferociously resisted both conquest and assimilation. In Iberia, the native population, ancestors of today's Portuguese, Castilian Spanish and Catalans, held out alongside the Basques in the northern mountains, and then began a tenacious 800-year recapture of their homeland known today as the Reconquista. Charles Martel crushed an Arab-led invasion force at Tours in 732, and as the latter was never accompanied by masses of migrants, the victory proved permanent and decisive. The Byzantine empire, regrouping after its initial defeat, held the Arabs back in Anatolia. It survived two enormous sieges of its capital, Constantinople, by the full might of the Caliphate in 674 and 717, and defended Europe's eastern border for another seven hundred years until finally succumbing to the Ottoman Turks.

If there is one clear lesson to be learned from the Arab conquests, it is that resistance means cultural survival. Surrender means cultural extinction.

There have been three great waves of Islamic expansion. The first was under the Rashidun Caliphate, which consisted of the first four caliphs to succeed Muhammad. The Rashidun conquests took place in a relatively short period of time, from 637 to 654 AD, and brought Syria, Armenia, Egypt, North Africa, and Cyprus under control of the Caliphate. The Byzantine-Arab wars also began during the Rashidun period, but would continue for another 116 years.

After the fourth Caliph, Ali ibn Abi Talib, was assassinated in the fifth year of his reign, in 661, a new dynasty known as the Ummayad Caliphate arose. (It is worth noting that the primary point of contention between Shi'a Muslims and Sunni Muslims revolves around the fourth Caliph; the Shi'ites are considered partisans of Ali and do not recognize the first three Rashidun caliphs.) The Ummayads continued where their predecessors left off, spreading to the east, the west, and the north, and crossing the Straits of Gibraltar to conquer both Spain and Portugal. At its peak, the Ummayad Caliphate controlled over 5 million square miles of territory; it is still the fifth-largest empire in world history.

The Ummayads were overthrown in 750 by the Abbasid dynasty, but the first great wave of Islamic expansion had already ended. The Abbasids were less known for their conquests than for their prosperity; the Golden Age of Islam is said to have begun with the reign of the Abbasid Caliph Harun al-Rashid in 786.

The second great wave of Islamic expansion began with a small principality in the Seljuk Sultanate of Rum. In 1299, Osman Bey declared independence from the Seljuks, who were a Turko-Persian empire that stood at the forefront of a Muslim world that had been weakened by the establishment of the Crusader states as well as Mongol incursions from the east. Osman drove the Byzantines out of Anatolia while fostering good relations with his Turkish neighbors, and although the Beylik of

Ottoman was still smaller than its neighbors at the time of his death in 1326, he had laid the foundations for an empire that would last 600 years, rule over 15 million people, and span three continents.

In 1389, Murad I defeated the Serbians and claimed southeastern Europe as vassal states of the Ottoman Empire. He also laid claim to the caliphate, a claim that was gradually recognized across the Muslim world. His great-great grandson, Mehmed the Conquerer, finished off the Byzantine Empire in 1453 by taking Constantinople, while Selim I expanded the empire into Persia and Egypt sixty years later. The Ottoman expansion did not stop until Suleiman the Magnificent failed twice before the gates of Vienna in 1529 and 1532, while the Battle of Lepanto in 1571 marked the turning point in the long struggle between Christendom and the Turk.

By the time the Grand Vizier Kara Mustafa Pasha was turned back from Vienna for a third and final time in 1683 by Christian forces led by the King of Poland, Jan Sobieski, the decline of the Ottoman Empire had already begun. The so-called "sick man of Europe" lingered on for another two centuries, but it largely ceased to be a Great Power in anything but name. The last Ottoman Caliph, Abdülmecid II, was formally deposed by Mustafa Kemal, the first President of the Turkish Republic, and the office was constitutionally abolished in 1924.

However, the expansion of the Turks had already changed this region of the world forever. From approximately the third millennium BC to 500 AD, most of central Asia was inhabited by nations genetically related to modern Persians and Europeans. Mummies were found that date back to that time include many with blonde, red, and light brown hair. As late as 600 AD, depictions of the Tocharian people of the Tarim basin in what is now western China show them with light-colored hair and eyes. And in Anatolia, the population was primarily Indo-European, including Greeks, Armenians, and others. Today, thanks to immigration, war, and ethnic cleansing, the region is now almost entirely inhabited by Turkic peoples speaking Turkish languages.

Both the Ottoman Empire and the Islamic Caliphate came to an end in the early 20th century. But even as the last ripples of the second great wave of Islamic expansion died out, the seeds of the third great wave had already been planted. In 1915, the lands of the Salafist ruler of Riyadh, Abdulaziz ibn Faisal, better known in the West as Ibn Saud, became a protectorate of the British Empire under the Treaty of Darin. The 1938 discovery of oil in the new kingdom of Saudi Arabia rapidly transformed what had been a minor desert backwater into a wealthy global player that also happened to be dedicated to a formerly obscure form of Islamic fundamentalism. As a result, the money that Saudi oil brought in was used to fund Islamic expansion around the world, as the Saudis have spent over $100 billion building mosques and madrassas around the world.

In December 2009, Hillary Clinton, then U.S. Secretary of State, went so far as to say, "Saudi Arabia remains a critical financial support base for al-Qaeda, the Taliban, LeT (Lashkar e-Tayyiba), and other terrorist groups, including Hamas."

Saudi oil money is why Salafism, a relatively minor branch of Sunni Islam that professed by only 4 percent of the Muslims in the Persian Gulf compared to the 23 percent Sunni minority and the 73 percent Shia majority, is growing explosively in the West. This fundamentalist form of Islamic orthodoxy, also known pejoratively as Wahhabism, is not only professed by most of the jihadists from the older groups, but is also the ideological fuel behind the Islamic State of Iraq and the Levant, better known as ISIL or ISIS.

What separates ISIS from older Islamic groups such as the Muslim Brotherhood, al-Qaeda, Hamas, Hezbollah, the Taliban, Boko Haram, and the Palestine Liberation Organization is not the way it utilizes social media or revels in almost cartoonish violence, but rather how it regards itself as the revived caliphate. On June 29, 2014, Abu Bakr al-Baghdadi declared that the Islamic State in Iraq and Greater Syria was now the true caliphate, and as such, it possessed religious, political and military authority over all Muslims worldwide. "The legality of all emirates, groups, states, and organisations, becomes null by the expansion of the khilāfah's authority and arrival of its troops to their areas." Al-Baghdadi's declaration marked the reestablishment of Islam in the eyes of jihadists around the world, and can be seen in the historical sense as being loosely akin to the famous call for crusade by Pope Urban II.

While it is common for more moderate Muslims in the West to deny the caliphate's authority and claim that the actions of its jihadists are "against Islam", the fact is that the caliphate's theology is both deeply learned and historically sound, and it is the moderates whose religion can be more legitimately questioned.

Many mainstream Muslim organizations have gone so far as to say the Islamic State is, in fact, un-Islamic. It is, of course, reassuring to know that the vast majority of Muslims have zero interest in replacing Hollywood movies with public executions as evening entertainment. But Muslims who call the Islamic State un-Islamic are typically, as the Princeton scholar Bernard Haykel, the leading expert on the group's theology, told me, "embarrassed and politically correct, with a cotton-candy view of their own religion" that neglects "what their religion has historically and legally required." Many denials of the Islamic State's religious nature, he said, are rooted in an "interfaith-Christian-nonsense tradition."

—"What ISIS Really Wants", Graeme Wood, *The Atlantic*, March 2015

At this point, it is impossible to determine the extent of this third great wave of Islamic expansion; based on the previous two there can be little doubt that it will attempt once more to conquer the West. Already over one million Muslims have been welcomed by the national leaders of Europe and the United States, whose populations are already 6 percent and 1.5 percent Muslim. Whether this third wave will be again turned back or not by a Christendom that has largely lost its faith will likely depend upon the men of the West returning to Christianity and regaining their cultural confidence.

Nous somme Charlie, but are we Charlie Hebdo or Charles Martel?

It is a common assumption on the part of most now living in the West that the technological advantages of our societies renders them militarily invulnerable. After all, for over 200 years, Western armies have repeatedly trounced less technologically well-equipped enemies, even when vastly outnumbered. What can a few thousand, even a few million barbarians intent on ruling over the world according to a 7th-century legal system possibly hope to accomplish against tolerant, secular, scientific societies that have split the atom, mapped the human genome, and landed on the Moon? How can machine guns crudely mounted on the backs of pickup trucks possibly defeat combat drones, directed high-energy weapons, nuclear cruise missiles, and air, space, and sea supremacy?

The uncomfortable reality is that throughout history, it is the less advanced societies who have frequently defeated their more sophisticated, more civilized opponents whose societies they are invading. The migrating Israelites conquered Canaan despite its walled cities. The Mongols overran a considerably more advanced Chinese society. The naval neophytes of Rome defeated Carthage, the mistress of the Mediterranean, and they defeated her at sea. Centuries later, the Roman Empire was invaded in turn eventually sacked by Germanic tribes that had been wearing animal skins and living in wooden huts when they first encountered the legions of Rome. And neither walls nor wealth nor one thousand years of civilization were sufficient to save Constantinople from the Ottoman Turks.

Mobility is the not-so-secret weapon of the less advanced, and immigration renders most, if not all, of the advantages possessed by the civilized societies moot. Walls cannot defend against barbarians that are already inside them. Nuclear weapons are useless against an enemy that is already living next door. France is a nuclear power, but even in light of the Bataclan massacre they cannot respond by nuking the infamous Belgian municipality of Molenbeek-Saint-Jean. And it is difficult for a society to work up the will to defeat the invader when the invader primarily appears in the form of little children walking to school, women shopping for their families in the markets, and the smiling faces of hard-working street vendors instead of faceless white figures on a black-and-white targeting screen.

And yet, the fact is that in terms of both the historical reality and the long-term consequences, there is essentially no difference between immigration and war. As Clausewitz famously said, "war is not merely an act of policy but a true political instrument, a continuation of political intercourse carried on with other means." And what other means is more effective than the demographic change wrought by mass immigration? As history testifies, the consequences of immigration in sufficient numbers are often considerably more damaging to a society, to a culture, or to a nation than the loss of a serious war. Japan lost an estimated 2.4 million nationals in World War II, but it remained Japan. 2.8 million Germans died in World War I, followed by another 4.2 million only 25 years later in World War II, but it remained identifiably German.

Will the same be said of Germany by the time the third great wave of Islamic expansion ends? Only time will tell. But the fate of all the invaded nations now lost to history, and the more than 200 American Indian tribes from the Ababco to the Wampanoag that are now extinct due to immigration, should serve as a warning to Europeans and Americans alike.

In a landmark essay for the military science fiction anthology *There Will Be War Vol. X*, Israeli military historian Martin van Creveld considered the history of both war and migration dating back to the dawn of recorded history before reaching the conclusion that they were, very often, one and the same:

> *Insofar as ancient war frequently involved not only soldiers and armies, but entire nations who left their homeland "mit man und Ross und wagen" (with man and horse and wagon), as the Germans say, war was migration. At some times, war and migration were essentially the same, as in the great migration of peoples during the first few centuries after Christ, the Arab expansion after 632 AD, the Magyar invasion of Europe, the Mongol invasions of China, and the movements of many African tribes from one part of the continent to another. At other times, the relationships between the two phenomena were more complicated, such as ethnic cleansings that rendered war unnecessary or took place after war's end, the mass avoidance of conscription, or soldiers bringing home concubines and war brides. All these various forms have often intermingled, all appear regularly in the annals of human history, and all will doubtless continue to do so in the future. The only thing that changes is their relative importance at any given point in time.*

> —"War and Migration", Martin van Creveld, 2015

Chapter 9

Christianity and Cuckservatism

The reason migrants without proper documentation are called illegal has nothing to do with their character, or their moral framework; they are illegal because those in power have the legislative authority to impose their definitions on society. When such laws restrict humans to participate in their full humanity, it is not the individual who is illegal; rather it is the prevailing laws that rob a certain group of people of their dignity that are illegal. And as such, Christians have a moral obligation to disobey such illegal laws. Immoral laws are usually ignored, not out of disrespect for the rule of law, but because the lack of justice erodes compliance. When the people continuously disregard the law, it indicates a lack of consent; and without the consent of the public, laws ceases to hold society together. For this reason, Christians realize that justice and equality toward the least always trumps any laws of nations that disenfranchise portions of the community.

Whenever immoral laws are in place, a moral obligation ex-
ists to be illegal.

—Miguel de la Torre, Professor of Social Ethics, Iliff
School of Theology

For the reader who is not a Christian, and who considers the Bible to be nothing more than just another ancient text, this chapter will likely strike you as irrelevant at best, and a digression into superstitious babble at worst. But because Christian organizations play such a massively influential role in American immigration, and because immigration advocates, both Christian and non-Christian, regularly appeal to Christian morality and specific Bible verses to justify their pro-immigration policies, it is important to at least be familiar with the conventional arguments that are presented on these issues under a nominally Christian guise even if one is a nonbeliever.

And if some of this pro-immigration theology strikes you as bizarre, well, let us assure you that much of it strikes us that way too. Bear with us and keep in mind that just as not all that glitters is gold, not all that calls itself Christian is, in fact, even remotely connected to genuine historical Christian theology.

Some years ago at a Baptist-affiliated church in Minnesota, a white man performed an unusual ritual. He got on his knees before the black music leader and tearfully begged the man's forgiveness for the historical sin committed by his white American ancestors in enslaving the music leader's African ancestors.

The music leader, on behalf of all black Americans past and present, raised the white man to his feet and announced that he (and presumably all black Americans), accepted the white man's (and presumably white America's) repentance, forgave him on behalf of all black Americans past and present, and the two men embraced. About two-thirds of the congregation immediately rose to their feet applauding both men, and more than a few tears were surreptitiously wiped away from more than a few eyes.

It was apparently, in the glistening eyes of many, a deeply touching moment.

The other one-third of the congregation sat there in disbelief, incredulous at the arrogant inanity of the ludicrous church theater. For some, it took a heroic amount of self-control to restrain the laughter that threatened to burst forth at the absurd racial self-flagellation on display.

God help us.

It is very important to understand that the two men on stage, the pastor and the music leader, were neither fools nor self-seeking attention whores. They are good Christian men whose devotion to God and Jesus Christ could not be more genuine. They are two of the finest, most decent men one could reasonably imagine. And it is because they are such good men that they serve so well to illustrate how bad theology, combined with an explicitly anti-Biblical and overtly non-Christian desire to repair the world, has gradually transformed the evangelical Church in America into a stronghold of irrational Churchian cuckservatism.

The absurdity of the racial forgiveness ritual was evident at the time, but time has only magnified the fact of its complete irrelevance. Has black America ceased to hold white America responsible for slavery? Have blacks abandoned their call for reparations? Have whites ceased to feel white guilt over the crimes of historical individuals to whom many of them are not even remotely related?

Of course not, which retroactively renders the entire performance moot.

This strange Christian perspective towards racial matters is not, strictly speaking, limited to cuckservatism, because it spans the entire American political spectrum from left to right. While most of the congregation of the church in which the racial theater took place tended to be conservative, as a general rule, it is the liberal churches that are even more concerned with worldly matters such as race, diversity, social justice, and immigration than they are with traditional Biblical or theological matters.

The main difference is that Christian churches that lean to the political right tend to fetishize the U.S. military, the American flag and the State of Israel, in many cases going so far as to fly the Israeli flag inside the sanctuary. Christian churches that lean to the political left are more inclined to elevate the current social justice narrative above the Gospel; it is not uncommon at such churches to hear sermons that quote more Marx than the Bible.

What may not be clear from outside the church is that the American Christian perspective on immigration is entirely driven by Christian sensitivities to the racial relations between black and white Americans. From the average American Christian's perspective, there is no substantive difference between African-Americans, Nigerians, Chinese, Pakistanis, Arabs, Haitians, Brazilians, Papua New Guineans, and Eskimos, as their ethnic spectrum consists of Whites (American), Whites (European), God's Chosen People (Jews), and Not-Whites (Blacks).

So, any opposition to unlimited immigration is inevitably seen as racism, because it involves not wanting Not-Whites to move in next door and Not-Whites are essentially Black for all intents and purposes. This may sound ridiculous, but you'll simply have to trust us on this one. There is nothing, literally *nothing*, that evangelicals love more than going on mission trips to Not-White countries in order to build homes, schools, and churches for underprivileged Not-White people. In the mission tripper's mind, he is a brave missionary going out to selflessly risk his life, preach the word of God, and convey the blessings of Christian civilization to a benighted, godless people in the mode of William Carey, David Livingstone and Hudson Taylor. If the benighted, godless people happen to be living in a sunny location near some nice beaches, so much the better.

It would surely be excessively cynical to observe how many of these missions from cold Midwestern states go to Belize, Jamaica, or the Dominican Republic in February, whereas in the summer, missions to uncivilized pagan settlements such as London are more common.

And while this desire to help the less fortunate and the Hell-bound no doubt flows genuinely from more generous hearts than ours, we would be remiss if we failed to note that there is no dearth of similarly godless poor in every major city in America. Yet somehow, it is deemed more virtuous for the young middle-class Christian to fly to a highly Catholic foreign country and attempt to evangelize a population containing a higher percentage of Christians than can be found on any university campus in America.

Many churches have reduced Christianity to the parable of the Good Samaritan, to such an extent that their religion could be more reasonably described as Good Samaritanism than Christianity. And while they subscribe chiefly to salvation through works and societally-approved attitudes rather than faith, they nevertheless possess complete and utter faith in the intrinsic goodness of foreigners.

Consider this passionate attack on the straightforward legal description of foreign individuals who have entered the country and remain resident in it without bothering to go through the legal niceties as "illegal immigrants" by Sojourners, a left-wing Christian group.

As the Senate recently passed long awaited immigration overhaul and the bill now heads to the House, the long-standing national discourse on the issue of immigration will likely heat up again. As we participate in these discussions, my hope is that we, especially as Christians tasked with peacemaking and reconciling, will find ways to build bridges instead of erecting walls. As a first step in this bridge building, I pray that once and for all, we will stop using the term "illegal immigrant."

Here's why:

1. *The term "illegal immigrant" is a misleading and dishonest term, which violates the 9th commandment.*

2. *The term "illegal" singles out those who committed one, specific, federal misdemeanor, but is never applied to other violations.*

3. *The term "illegal immigrant" has morphed into a racial epithet.*

4. *The term "illegal immigrant" cultivates hostility, animosity, and mistrust against our neighbors.*

5. *The term "illegal immigrant" is dehumanizing.*

This nominally Christian argument is factually false as well as a perversion of both Scripture and the English language.

1. "Illegal immigrant" is an accurate and honest legal term that precisely describes the status of the individual. If someone has left his native country for another one, he is an immigrant. If he does so outside the procedures defined by the law, he has immigrated illegally. Therefore, he is an illegal immigrant. It is not bearing false witness to describe another individual accurately in this matter, in fact, it is bearing true witness. There is nothing misleading or dishonest about the term "illegal immigrant".

2. Murder and rape are also federal crimes. Anyone who has committed one of them, even once, is customarily known as a "murderer" or a "rapist". The statement is obviously false.

3. "Illegal immigrant" is not a racist epithet. To what race does "illegal immigrant" refer? According to the Pew Research Center, 15.2 percent of illegal immigrants come from Central America, 12.4 percent from Asia, 6.3 percent from South America, 5.3 percent from Europe, and 3.5 percent from the Middle East and Canada.

4. It's not the term "illegal immigrant" that cultivates hostility, animosity, and mistrust against our neighbors, but rather the invasion of 60 million foreigners over the last 50 years.

5. There is nothing dehumanizing about the term as only humans are described as "illegal immigrants". Have you ever heard of migrating birds or whales being described that way? Neither have we.

As can be seen from the analysis of the argument presented above, these Churchians (for it would not be strictly accurate to describe them as Christians) are liars and deceivers. They worship the god of Babel, not the Christian God. They serve the world, not Jesus Christ, as can be seen in their articulation of their mission and their vision.

Our Mission: We seek to inspire hope and build a movement to transform individuals, communities, the church, and the world.

Our Vision: We envision a future in which Christians put their faith into action in the passionate pursuit of social justice, peace, and environmental stewardship, working in partnership with people of other perspectives, for the common good

of communities, families and individuals. We articulate that
vision, convene and mobilize constituencies, and build al-
liances for effective advocacy.

The Sojourners even prominently feature a diversity statement that is "in accordance with Sojourners' mission to articulate the biblical call to social justice" and commit themselves to "confront and dismantle discriminatory behavior wherever it may be manifest."

As with the more conservative Baptist-affiliated church mentioned above, these left-wing Churchians are far more inclined to confront discriminatory behavior than any of the mortal or venial sins chronicled in the Bible. As for the nonexistent "biblical call to social justice" (and it is all too telling that the word "biblical" is not capitalized), it flies in the face of the genuine Christian call to be in the world, not of it.

But where does this religious obsession with improving the world through works come from, when it has been absent from Christian theology for the greater part of two thousand years? Indeed, the entire conceptual core of Christianity is fundamentally based on the nature of the world not only being fallen and imperfect and ruled by an immortal spirit of evil, but remaining that way until the Son returns, the Prince of the World is cast down, and the Kingdom of Heaven is established.

Justice, in both Greek philosophy and proper Christian theology, is "rectitude of the will", as can be seen in Aquinas's *Summa Theologica*, specifically Secunda Secundæ Partis, Question 58, Article 1. And in the Christian sense, rectitude of the will is defined by conformity with God's will, which can be debated, but being immutable, is assuredly not defined by the ever-mutating social justice narrative.

So social justice Christianity, or Good Samaritanism, or Churchianity, all amount to the same thing: a false form of Christianity that cloaks itself in Christian rhetoric while denying both the conceptual core of Christianity and the fundamental nature of the justice to which it nominally dedicates itself. And these false forms all flow from a concept that is considerably newer than Christianity, although it is related to an older religion.

The term *tikkun olam* is from the rabbinic literature known as the Mishnah, which dates back to 1492 and is believed to come from an oral tradition that may be as much as a thousand years older. It appears in the phrase *mip'nei tikkun ha-olam* "to indicate that a practice should be followed not because it is required by Biblical law, but because it helps avoid social disharmony."

The phrase is often translated as "for the sake of the healing of the world", which is why the expression appears in English as a directive to "heal the world" or "fix the world", but a better translation is "for the sake of the perfection of the world".

In other words, the cuckservatives and other Churchians have elevated a literally extra-Biblical post-Christian concept that flies directly in the face of genuine Christian theology to a super-Scriptural level, then used it as the basis to judge both members of the Church and the Bible itself!

The Great Evangelical Cuckoo Hunt

The effects of this theological confusion go considerably beyond the aforementioned teen mission trips to impoverished, but sunny lands near the equator. Of late, evangelicals in particular have embraced transracial adoption as a new Christian virtue, with the amount of virtue endowed by the adoptee primarily dependent upon the color of his skin. Rachel Dolezal, the infamous trans-black President of the Spokane Branch of the NAACP, is one example of a child raised by white Christian evangelicals who adopted four black children; the *Huff-*

ington Post described her parents thusly:

> *Dolezal's biological parents, Ruthanne and Larry, are deeply*
> *conservative evangelical Christians whose faith has inspired*
> *them to personally seek out ways to redeem and save human-*
> *ity—whether it's by evangelizing on a mission trip or bringing*
> *four adopted black children into their home. "[Rachel's] social*
> *justice advocacy is just a carry-over of the values within her*
> *home," Larry Dolezal told The Huffington Post on Tuesday.*

The Christian version is perhaps the most intensely distilled form of
cuckservatism, as the seeking out of these cuckoo children is not only
preached from the pulpits, but even modeled by the pastors. Kathryn
Joyce, a critic of the evangelical adoption movement and author of *The
Child Catchers: Rescue, Trafficking, and the New Gospel of Adoption*, explains that, like the racial theater described earlier in this chapter, transracial adoption is one way in which white Christians attempt to expiate
their guilt for their imaginary historical sins against African-Americans:

> *Some evangelicals are approaching transracial adoption as a*
> *means of "racial reconciliation": a way for historically white*
> *evangelical churches to diversify and become more like the*
> *"rainbow congregations" they wish they were. One move-*
> *ment leader, Russell Moore of the Southern Baptist Conven-*
> *tion, described adoption as equivalent to the Civil Rights*
> *Movement—a movement that Moore said his denomination*
> *had ignored during the 1960s, to its shame. In a way, he*
> *was arguing that adopting transracially was a chance for the*
> *church to get it right on racial issues after failing so badly in*
> *the past.*

It never seems to occur to these white guilt-trippers that holding today's
white Christians responsible for the sins of their 18th-century or 1960s

counterparts is no different than blaming today's Jews for crucifying Jesus Christ.

But transtemporal collective guilt complexes are not the only justification for transracial adoptions. Evangelicals who have adopted transracially also like to point to a particular Bible verse as justification for their actions.

> *Religion that God our Father accepts as pure and faultless is this: to look after orphans and widows in their distress and to keep oneself from being polluted by the world.*
>
> —James 1:27

One sees this reference over and over again amongst Christian cuckservatives. Consider, for example, the words of one Presbyterian family about their two transracial adoptions: "We see our two adoptions as natural outgrowths of obedience to God's Word. As Christians, we are to care for the fatherless and orphans. If we have the resources and gifts we should consider God's calling to adopt."

But there are better ways to provide for orphans than to displace one's own children; we tend to doubt that the average Christian wife would accept the same Scriptural argument on behalf of bringing a widowed woman into one's home, particularly if she happened to be young and attractive. Moreover, if one is to keep oneself from being polluted by the world, how can these adoptions, or any other action inspired by social justice, be justified on the basis of perfecting that very world?

Another verse that is very popular with social-justice-minded Christians, particularly with regards to adoption and immigration, is Galatians 3:28, which states:

> *There is neither Jew nor Gentile, neither slave nor free, nor is there male and female, for you are all one in Christ Jesus.*

Now, this is obviously a reference to spiritual equality before God rather than a denial of observable Earthly differences. And I have yet to see any Christian who makes a habit of resorting to this verse to defend immigration accept it as a basis for denying the legitimacy of the State of Israel or eliminating sex-segregated bathrooms and showers.

As is often the case, the true motivator of the Christian cuckservative can be seen in his language. As evangelical adoption critics David and Desiree Smolin have noted in "The Liberal Roots of the Modern Adoption Movement", "pro-transracial adoption rhetoric is fundamentally pro-equality, integrationist and multi-cultural rhetoric."

In other words, the primary driver of Christian cuckservatism is not Christian at all. But to the extent that transracial adoption is influenced by Christianity, it is the result of the same erroneous theological perspective as the racial and immigration aspects, namely, Jesus Christ's penultimate command to love one's neighbor as oneself. But who, precisely, is one's neighbor?

This, as most Bible-reading Christians will know, leads us back to the parable of the Good Samaritan from Luke 10:25–37. The parable is frequently cited by Christians and non-Christians alike to justify everything from government transfer payments to forcibly imposing refugees on protesting U.S. States.

The Parable of the Good Samaritan

> On one occasion an expert in the law stood up to test Jesus. "Teacher," he asked, "what must I do to inherit eternal life?"
>
> "What is written in the Law?" he replied. "How do you read it?"
>
> He answered, " 'Love the Lord your God with all your heart

and with all your soul and with all your strength and with all your mind'; and, 'Love your neighbor as yourself.'"

"You have answered correctly," Jesus replied. "Do this and you will live."

But he wanted to justify himself, so he asked Jesus, "And who is my neighbor?"

In reply Jesus said: "A man was going down from Jerusalem to Jericho, when he was attacked by robbers. They stripped him of his clothes, beat him and went away, leaving him half dead. A priest happened to be going down the same road, and when he saw the man, he passed by on the other side. So too, a Levite, when he came to the place and saw him, passed by on the other side. But a Samaritan, as he traveled, came where the man was; and when he saw him, he took pity on him. He went to him and bandaged his wounds, pouring on oil and wine. Then he put the man on his own donkey, brought him to an inn and took care of him. The next day he took out two denarii and gave them to the innkeeper. 'Look after him,' he said, 'and when I return, I will reimburse you for any extra expense you may have.'

"Which of these three do you think was a neighbor to the man who fell into the hands of robbers?"

The expert in the law replied, "The one who had mercy on him."

Jesus told him, "Go and do likewise."

The Good Samaritan did help the man. But he helped him by giving the man some of his own money, not by using the king's soldiers to take money away from other people, taking a cut himself, and giving the rest to the man. He put the man up in an inn; he did not move the man into his house, provide him with room and board, then permit the man to send for his wife, his children, his parents, and his cousins, and let them move in and live off the largesse of the other people in his neighborhood while raping their children, stealing their cars, and trashing their yards.

To have mercy on foreigners in need is not to pay for them to literally become your neighbor and move in next door to you and live off the welfare state.

The genuine Christian position on refugees, immigrants, and people from other lands is to be found in the Book of Matthew.

> *Leaving that place, Jesus withdrew to the region of Tyre and Sidon. A Canaanite woman from that vicinity came to him, crying out, "Lord, Son of David, have mercy on me! My daughter is demon-possessed and suffering terribly."*
>
> *Jesus did not answer a word. So his disciples came to him and urged him, "Send her away, for she keeps crying out after us."*
>
> *He answered, "I was sent only to the lost sheep of Israel."*
>
> *The woman came and knelt before him. "Lord, help me!" she said.*
>
> *He replied, "It is not right to take the children's bread and toss it to the dogs."*
>
> —Matthew 15:21–26

Now, Jesus himself made an exception to the rule for the woman's sake, due to her exceptional faith. But she was an exception, and the exception does not change the rule. It is certainly good and right to help people from other nations with "the crumbs that fall from their master's table". It will not harm a wealthy nation with budget surplus and no pressing domestic needs to send foreign aid to other countries.

But that is no longer the case these days. And to do more is to deprive our posterity, which Jesus himself said is not right.

The False Fruit of Churchianity

How can we know what is right and what is not from the Christian perspective? As it happens, we have been left with instructions in this regard. The most important spiritual test of the Christian legitimacy of any interpretation of Scripture is the consequential one recommended by Jesus in the Sermon on the Mount.

> *Watch out for false prophets. They come to you in sheep's cloth-*
> *ing, but inwardly they are ferocious wolves. By their fruit you*
> *will recognize them. Do people pick grapes from thornbushes,*
> *or figs from thistles? Likewise, every good tree bears good fruit,*
> *but a bad tree bears bad fruit. A good tree cannot bear bad*
> *fruit, and a bad tree cannot bear good fruit. Every tree that*
> *does not bear good fruit is cut down and thrown into the fire.*
> *Thus, by their fruit you will recognize them.*
>
> —Matthew 7:15–20

Churchianity in general, and Good Samaritanism in particular, reliably fail this test. It is worth noting that the pro-immigration Churchians almost always exhibit a defiant lawlessness in the service of social justice cloaked in pseudo-Christian babble.

> *I plan to love and welcome anyone and everyone, regardless of*
> *legal status. My allegiance is first and foremost to the King-*
> *dom of God, and in God's government acceptance is preemi-*
> *nent. Join me in loving immigrants and learning from them*

as we hope for immigration reform that results in a more just
and equitable treatment of all people in this country.

—John March, Lead Pastor, New City Covenant Church

It strikes us as more than a little strange to insist that that the same Creator God who ordered the slaughter of the Canaanites and the Amalekites, condemned Jeroboam for his tolerance, makes a point of separating the sheep from the goats as well as the wheat from the chaff, and sends the wicked and the unbeliever to Hell, places a particular priority on "acceptance". Is John March preaching genuine Christian doctrine or is he a ferocious wolf in sheep's clothing? We trust even the non-Christian reader is capable of discernment here.

One reader wrote about a Churchian family he knew that decided Good Samaritanism, in its James 1:27 form, was the proper form of charity. The family invited into their home a 24-year-old woman with a baby who had walked out on her husband, claiming that she had been abused. The idea was that the mother and child would live with the good samaritans for a few months while she got back on her feet and got her life back together.

Within a year their family was destroyed. The charity case was pregnant with the husband's child, and the wife filed for divorce.

By their fruit you will recognize them.

Lesson: don't take charity cases into your home. This is as true for nations as it is for families.

The false fruit of Churchian multiculturalism can be recognized by what is happening to Christian churches everywhere from Europe to the American Midwest. So-called Christians are not only actively welcoming those who do not worship Jesus Christ to invade their nations, they are also watering down Christian theology and in some cases, literally tearing down the symbols of Christian worship. In Germany, a

Lutheran Church in Hamburg has been converted into a mosque. In France, 60 churches have been closed in the last decade while 150 new mosques are under construction. In Spain, the Stations of the Cross were removed from the pilgrimage church of Nuestra Señora del Roble in Cenicientos due to the lack of respect the stone steles showed those who "profess the Muslim religion and culture" by virtue of their very existence.

And at North Heights Lutheran Church in Minnesota, where one of the author's parents attended for years, a female pastor has driven two-thirds of the former parishioners out of the church due to their "bigotry" and "sexism", and has announced her vision to integrate Muslims and Christians in a new progressive church called "Chrislam".

By their fruit you will recognize them.

It is not right to take the children's bread and toss it to the dogs.

Chapter 10

A Challenge to the Cuckservative

Today, in Europe, we do not find ourselves facing a phenomenon of immigration. We find ourselves facing a phenomenon of migration. It feels like an immigration, but it is a migration, a historic event of incalculable scope. They do not travel in such a horde that the grass will no longer grow where their horses have trampled, but in discrete clusters that attract little notice; nevertheless, the process will take not centuries or millenia but decades. And like all the great migrations, it will finally result in a rearrangement of the ethnicity of the land of their destination, an inexorable change of costumes, an unstoppable hybridization that noticeably mutates the color of the skin, the hair and the eyes of the population, as even a small number of Normans left behind their blond hair and blue eyes in Sicily.... The great migrations cannot be stopped.

We simply must prepare ourselves to live in a new season of Afro-European culture.

—Umberto Eco, "Migrazioni", *La Bustina di Minerva*, 1990. Trans. Vox Day

As with all intellectual concepts, the intrinsic wrongness of cuckservatism can be observed in the false nature of its foundations. Its philosophy is illogical, its predictive models are empirically incorrect, its theology is anti-Biblical, and its consequences are societally destructive. When its premises and rationales are considered in detail, it soon becomes clear that only communism and feminism can rival cuckservatism in terms of being a more fallacious utopian ideology.

Despite their many contradictions, failed predictions, and disastrous consequences, both feminism and communism survive today as ideologies commanding the allegiance of millions. Is it possible that the treasonous ideology of cuckservatism will similarly survive to inflict itself on future generations of America?

No, it will not, because while both feminism and communism contain the seeds of their own destruction within them, multiple generations are required for the full effects of either to be realized. After all, there is a lot of ruin in a nation.

But whereas feminism and communism only affect the nature of the nation, cuckservatism strikes at the essence of the nation itself.

While feminism reduces marriage rates, birth rates, and wage rates, the negative effects on society are gradual; even after 40 years of near-complete feminist dominance, most Western societies are still in relatively mild demographic decline as the inherent maternal instinct tends to mitigate the influence of feminism. And although communism eradicates the price mechanism necessary for the operation of supply and demand, and warps the incentives for capital and labor alike, the inevitable development of black markets so successfully balances the negative economic effects that it took 70 years for communism to implode the Soviet Union.

Had it not been for the foolish decision of the Soviets to attempt to keep up with the military spending of the capitalist West, communism might have even limped along for another decade or three.

Cuckservatism, on the other hand, has already presented an existential threat to the United States of America in barely half the time it took communism to bring about the collapse of the Soviet Union. The threat it poses is particularly insidious because its effects not only strike society on multiple levels, but tend to exacerbate each other. As free trade impoverishes the nation and immigration changes both the culture and the demographics, the resulting loss of cultural confidence and despair inspire the younger generation to begin imitating the invaders, thereby further weakening the traditional bonds of the nation. Religious and ethnic differences widen the gap between various groups, which begin competing for resources and transform the political system into a straightforward racial spoils system.

This is hardly a new story. The same pattern of war followed by migration followed by war has been repeated over and over and over again, in every part of the world. From Austria-Hungary to Yugoslavia, multi-ethnic states have always eventually returned to a semblance of homogeneity through various means both fair and foul.

What is new is the scale of the migration. The 50-year mass migration into the United States is the single largest invasion in human history. At over 60 million, it dwarfs Operation Barbarossa, in which Hitler sent 3.8 million men into the Soviet Union. It is *two orders of magnitude* larger than the Mongol horde of Batu Khan, which conquered over 2.3 million square miles of territory from Burma to Bulgaria. It is *one thousand times* larger than the First Crusade. And it is twice the number of immigrants who entered the United States between 1870 and 1930 and at the time, represented an estimated 60 percent of the entire world's immigrants.

It requires a near-complete ignorance of history to assume, as cuckservatives do, that an invasion of this magnitude will not have an extraordinary impact on the long-term fate of the United States, or that it does not represent an existential threat to the very survival of America as a nation.

The ever-dour prophet of doom, John Derbyshire, has forecast five possible fates for what he calls "the white world", by which he means the European nations, Australia, New Zealand, and the United States of America. In an article entitled "Five Scenarios for the White World", Derbyshire describes the five scenarios as follows:

1. Absorption. All will be well. The migrants, in whatever numbers choose to come, will enrich and energize our tired, aging societies. They will take on our liberal values and become good Europeans, Americans, and Canadians.

2. Restriction. Political pressure from their native populations will force receiving nations to stem the flow. Fences will go up, coastal patrols will commence; but those illegals who are in, will be allowed to stay in.

3. Rejection. There will be a real uprising of native peoples. Illegals will be deported en masse to their countries of origin.

4. Surrender. The native European and European-descended populations, enervated by soft living and psychologically disarmed by globalist propaganda, will yield up their societies to the invaders.

5. Fragmentation. Some part or parts of the First World will opt

for one of the foregoing scenarios, some other part or parts for a different one.

John Derbyshire sees scenario number 2, Restriction, as being the most likely outcome, but we regard all of these scenarios as being fundamentally too optimistic to be credible. Both the historical pattern and the trend of current events point to there being one more, considerably darker outcome, that is much more likely.

That outcome is civil war on a continental scale. Austria-Hungary collapsed after starting World War I with an invasion of Serbia. Yugoslavia collapsed into inter-ethnic, inter-religious civil war following the death of Tito, as has also happened across the Arab world as the strongmen who brutally suppressed tribal and religious differences in their countries were removed from power by the Western democracies. The Rwandan genocide was the result of the ethnic struggle between the Tutsi and Hutu tribes over the Rwandan government.

And what the results of that war will be cannot possibly be known. In 2014, the Islamic State successfully reestablished the caliphate for the first time since the death of Abdülmecid II in 1924 and it already has adherents pledging loyalty to it everywhere from the Philippines to Paris and Philadelphia. From its territory, it can offer fighters and logistical support to its soldiers throughout the Dār al-Harb, the House of War, as the rest of the world is known to it.

Even as we wrote this chapter, the Islamic State struck in Paris, killing 129 innocent civilians there, and followed that up by releasing a video threatening both Washington D.C. and New York City. Barely three weeks later, the jihad came to California, as a Pakistani immigrant who is reported to have publicly pledged allegiance to Caliph Abu Bakr al-Baghdadi killed 14 civilians in San Bernardino, California with her husband, a second-generation Pakistani immigrant.

Governors from U.S. States that possess 315 Electoral College votes have *openly* rebelled against the Obama administration's insistence that they accept some of the 12,200 Syrian "refugees" the Federal government has granted permission to immigrate. Hundreds of mosques and refugee centers are burning across Europe, and there has already been one assassination attempt of a pro-migration German politician. Multiple countries are violating or openly abrogating the Schengen Agreement. A popular nationalist meme has appeared on Twitter that features a picture of convicted Norwegian mass-murderer Anders Breivik with the caption "Free Me and I Will Free You."

The initial response of Western leaders to this widespread outrage has been to ignore popular anger and double down on their pro-immigration rhetoric. The politician arguably most culpable for the current European migrant crisis, Angela Merkel, the Chancellor of Germany, has responded to mass nationalist rallies featuring shocking images of gallows and accusations of treason with the same insipid multiculturalist mantra repeatedly heard from American cuckservatives:

> *She called on Germans to show their determination not to be intimidated, by standing up for the values of respecting the right of each individual to pursue happiness and of living together in respect and tolerance. 'We know that our life of freedom is stronger than terror,' she said. 'Let us answer the terrorists by living our values with courage.'*

—"Merkel Tells Germans, 'Freedom Is Stronger Than Terror'", the *New York Times*, 14 November 2015

French President Francois Hollande's reaction to the Paris attacks was even more difficult to believe, as he announced to a national gathering of mayors that France would accept 30,000 more Syrian "refugees" over the next two years—and received a standing ovation! It is not surprising that his nationalist rival, Marine Le Pen of the Front National, has risen rapidly in the polls and is widely expected to replace him after the next election.

President Obama's behavior has been no better. He has threatened to veto legislation that would strengthen the screening process prospective refugees must undergo and claimed that "slamming the door in the face of refugees would betray our deepest values", which makes one wonder precisely whose values he has in mind.

This feckless insistence on forcing even more immigration on the increasingly unwilling native populations by the politicians has led to the rise of nationalist parties across the West, as France's Front National, Germany's Alternative für Deutschland, Sweden's Sverigedemokraterna, Switzerland's Schweizerische Volkspartei, Greece's Golden Dawn, and the unlikely presidential candidacy of Donald Trump have all risen powerfully in the polls. And if the ruling pro-immigration parties attempt to change the rules in order to keep them out of power, as the Portuguese president unsuccessfully tried in October after the four leftist parties won a parliamentary majority, it is certain that even more extreme parties with no respect for democracy will rise in reaction to the anti-democratic shenanigans of the multiculturalists.

This book will not convince everyone. But we believe that we have presented a substantial and conclusive case for American nationalism that will convince every fair-minded reader who believes in America and the national interest of Americans. America is not a propositional nation, it is a distinct nation of people with their own customs, traditions, DNA, and culture, and it is *a nation that has the right to defend its own existence.*

The uncomfortable truth is that cuckservatism not only betrays America's posterity, it also betrays the intent of the other clauses of the Preamble to the Constitution, including, "to form a more perfect

Union", "establish Justice", "insure domestic Tranquility", "provide for the common defence", and "promote the General Welfare", five things that adding 60 million immigrants in 50 years have manifestly not done. One could make a very strong argument that thanks to their cuckservative ideology, America's self-styled conservatives have literally betrayed the entire purpose of the Constitution of the United States of America, and in doing so, they have put the very survival of the nation at risk.

So the question we would pose to the pro-immigration conservative, is this: is it really worth it?

The policies you have endorsed have made your country poorer, more dangerous, more crowded, and literally more stupid. What have you, personally, gained from 60 million immigrants that justifies even the most remote risk of the United States collapsing into a brutal Yugoslavia-style civil war? Are you not even a little bit troubled by the prospect of American blood being shed by those whose presence in your country you have not only cheered, but championed? Do you not, in your deepest heart of hearts, find yourself afraid of what is in store for this unrecognizable land that is no longer America and can no longer be described as a nation?

Perhaps not. Perhaps you genuinely believe the various changes you have championed are truly for the better. In that case, be warned, cuckservative. You may find the label to be insulting, perhaps even offensive, but if any of the darker scenarios we envision come to pass, you will surely be called worse. Quisling. Turncoat. Collaborator. Traitor.

Even now, it is not too late to learn to love your people, love your country, love your nation and stop betraying them in the interests of those who, at best, are taking advantage of you, and at worst, are actively planning your destruction. Even now, it is not to late to join the rising tide of American nationalism and take America back!

You may not like the label, cuckservative, but the fact is that you cannot reasonably call yourself an American conservative if you don't believe America, and the American people, are worth conserving. How much longer are you willing to play Wile E. Coyote to the left's Roadrunner? How much longer do you think you *can*?

As a wiser and better man than we are once said: "It is not right to take the children's bread and toss it to the dogs." It is not right, it is not moral, and it is not Constitutional to betray America's posterity.

America is under ongoing attack from the Globalist Left and the Corporate Right, both of whom have interests that are diametrically opposed to the American national interest. Americans must reclaim their country and defend their political traditions, their culture, and their ethnic nation, or they will eventually find themselves going the way of the American Indian and walking their own Trail of Tears.

Appendix A:

Interview with Vox Day

GREG JOHNSON: I'm Greg Johnson. Welcome to Counter-Currents Radio. My guest today is Vox Day. Vox, welcome to the show.

VOX DAY: Thanks, Greg, good to be here.

GJ: I recently discovered your work. I am ashamed to admit it, but your interests had not really intersected with mine until you published SJWs Always Lie, and my friend Ann Sterzinger wrote a review of it for Counter-Currents and I decided I would read you myself.

I thought this was a really excellent book, and it's on the required reading list for all of my readers. I'm expecting book reports in my in-box tomorrow morning from my inner circle, so to speak. They should all be reading it.

I wanted to just get to know you a little bit better, get to know your political philosophy, get to know how you became the author of this book. So, can you tell me a little bit about your worldview? How would you describe your political philosophy and who are some of the intellectual influences on its formation?

VD: I would describe myself as a Christian Western Civilizationist. I've been a libertarian for a long time. I was briefly even a card-carrying libertarian. But I was always more of a small L libertarian rather than a capital L one. Mostly because there were certain amounts of libertarian dogma that didn't quite work out in the real world. Then as time went on it became readily apparent to me as I traveled around the world, as I lived in different countries, as I learned different languages, it became apparent to me that the abstract ideals that we often tend to follow in America in particular are not really relevant to most of the world.

I was being interviewed by a reporter from *Le Monde* in Paris about two months ago and he had absolutely no idea how to even begin to describe the concept of libertarianism to his readers. That was in France, which is at least part of Western civilization. Trying to have a conversation about that sort of concept in Japan or China is just totally meaningless. So, that's when I really became more cognizant of the importance of the nationalist element of ideology.

I think that just as Stalin found it necessary to modify international socialism for the Russians, and just as Mao found it necessary to modify international socialism for the Chinese, it's necessary for the advocates of every other ideology to understand that there are nationalistic and tribalistic limits to the practical application of those abstract ideologies.

GJ: That's interesting. I'm an ex-libertarian myself. I was not a card-carrying libertarian, but I subscribed to *Reason* magazine and read lots of Ayn Rand and Hayek and Mises mostly when I was an undergraduate. There were things that led me away from that. Two books in particular. First, I read Thomas Sowell's *A Conflict of Visions* and the other was Céline's *Journey to the End of the Night*, which basically destroyed my liberal optimism about humanity.

What are some of the things that you think don't work about libertarianism? You said that some of the abstract libertarian dogmas just don't work, so specifically what are those?

VD: Well, the most important one, as we are now seeing, is the free movement of peoples. What really changed my thinking and it was a process, you know, it wasn't an immediate thing, although it was a fairly quick process now that I think about it. I grew up on Milton Friedman. My father had me reading *Free to Choose* when I was fairly young, and so I was a big free trade dogmatist and around the time of NAFTA and all that sort of thing I could recognize some of the problems but I bought into the line that the problem is that it's not real free trade. It's a free trade agreement, but it's not real free trade.

Then I read a really good book by Ian Fletcher in which he directly addressed the concept of Ricardo's comparative advantage, and he really destroyed it. I think he had some-

thing like seven major problems with it, and that got me
interested, so I started looking into it. I'm very fortunate
in that I have a pretty active and intelligent blog reader-
ship, they really like to engage, and they have absolutely
no respect for me, so they're quite happy to argue with me.

Most of them were free-traders as well, so we ended up
having an ongoing two- or three-week debate about free
trade, and it got pretty detailed, to the extent that I went
through Henry Hazlitt's entire chapter on free trade to
look at it critically rather than just reading through it and
accepting it at face value. Looking at the free trade arguments, I found that they were full of holes. Not just
Ricardo's, but Hazlitt's as well. That's what caused me to
realize that Ricardo's argument was totally dependent on
the idea that capital could move, but labor couldn't. So
what that got me thinking about was the fact that a libertarian society—even if we could convince everyone in
the United States that libertarianism was the correct way
to approach things—would rapidly be eliminated by the
free movement of peoples, as people from non-libertarian
societies, people from cultures where they have absolutely
no ideals that are in common with the Founding Fathers
or with libertarian ideals, would rapidly be able to come in
and end that libertarian society in much the same way that
the Californians have gone into Colorado and completely
changed the political climate there.

So, Ian Fletcher's book is what really triggered that whole
shift in thought process. Now I look at the concept of the
free movement of peoples, free trade, and those sorts of

concepts with a considerable amount of skepticism. Of course, in Europe we're seeing some of those problems related to the idea of the free movement of peoples just as you see it in the States with the Central Americans coming across the border.

GJ: Right. What is the name of the Fletcher book?

VD: Let me see here. Actually, I have it right here. It is *Free Trade Doesn't Work: What Should Replace It and Why*.

GJ: Okay. That's going to go right on my reading list. Thank you. There were two things that really undermined my libertarianism. One was very much what you were talking about. It simply occurred to me that a libertarian society requires people that are willing to play by that ethic, but if a libertarian society doesn't exclude people who will exploit that ethic then it will be destroyed. If you have open borders, and anybody can come in and basically they can come in and take your stuff or take your society from you, that will be the end of libertarianism. Therefore libertarianism requires that you exclude the free-riders, exclude the people who don't play by those rules. But you can't do that by libertarian means. You can't draw borders around people, you can't say, "You have to leave because you won't play by the rules of our game."

VD: Well, you can if you modify them. I think that the libertarian movement, if it is going to survive, is going to have to make the same shift that we saw with the Communist ideology, and it's going to need to shift from an interna-

GJ: tional libertarianism to a national libertarianism, because otherwise it simply can't survive.

GJ: Right.

VD: One of the authors that I publish at Castalia House is the Israeli military historian Martin van Creveld. He's absolutely brilliant. He's actually added to the military canon. You can't understand military events if you haven't read van Creveld.

The thing that's fascinating to me is we were talking and we have a military sci-fi, military fact anthology that we publish every year called *Riding the Red Horse* and so I called Martin up and said, "Hey, I'd really like you to contribute something, contribute an essay to it." And he said, "Yeah, okay. I'd love to." And he did. He sent in this phenomenal essay on migration and war. The really interesting thing about it—and keep in mind we're talking about a premier military historian here—is that historically speaking, migration is war and war is migration.

When the Helveti invaded the Gaulish lands and Caesar went and ended up defeating them after they had beaten the Roman legions previously, that was a movement of peoples. That was not just an army. And it's the same with the Goths; it's the same with the Huns; it's the same with the Mongols. These were not the equivalent of the German Wehrmacht marching across a border. This was the entire society on the move, and so the distinction that we make between immigration and war is really a relatively modern one, and it's largely an unofficial one as well.

[Note: "War and Migration" will NOT be appearing in *Riding the Red Horse Vol. 2*. Vox made the elementary mistake of mentioning the essay to Jerry Pournelle prior to publication, who read it and promptly stole it for *There Will Be War Vol. X*. Both military science fiction anthologies are published by Castalia House, so Vox is only mildly bitter about it.]

GJ: I would agree with that. I said this some years ago, I think, in an interview with Dennis Fetcho. We were talking about this very topic, and I said that looking at the late Roman Empire, looking at the barbarian invasions, these were not armies blitzing across borders. These are large migrations of people, and the Romans were constantly bringing these people in and settling them in their lands to work for them and fight for them and things like that. The Romans thought this was working out quite well for them right up until the point when it wasn't.

VD: Sure, and that's the problem, because it does work fine... for a while. It's connected to the same reason that central banks keep interest rates low and the same reason that kids don't do their homework until the night before. It is a normal human thing to put off the difficult task as long as possible, and unfortunately one way that a society can put off some of its problems, put off facing those problems, is by permitting large migrations to freely enter. Of course, the price of that is usually the eventual collapse of the society.

GJ: Right and in the short run it does serve short-term elite interests, which is why it's permitted in the first place. It's cheap labor, soldiers for the legions, whatever the motives were. Or just because it's easier to go along with this for a little while than raise an army and repulse it. Eventually though you find that you've been replaced in your own homeland.

When Rome was sacked it was sacked by people who were settled for generations inside the Roman Empire itself. It wasn't a long march for them to get to Rome and sack it.

VD: Right.

GJ: They were already there, and I think that looking at what's happening in Europe today and looking at the United States today it's exactly the same process.

VD: The ironic thing is that it's actually much worse in the USA than it is in Europe, even though people don't realize it, because most Americans don't understand that the Muslim population in Europe is about five percent. It's actually a little less than five percent. Whereas the Hispanic community in the United States is pushing 30 percent.

GJ: Right.

VD: And also the European nations have a much stronger, much more active sense of nationalism. You can't be German if... I was up in Cologne a few weeks ago and there was a Turkish gentleman who was my taxi driver. We were talking a bit and he had been in Germany for something like 27 years or 30 years or something and he still considered himself to be Turkish, whereas if someone has lived in the States for 30 years people say, "Oh, you're an American. You're an American now." Whereas the Germans would never reach that conclusion.

GJ: Right. This almost sounds like the beginning of a stand-up routine, but whenever I get into a cab I always ask the immigrant what country he's from, and they always tell me, and then I always ask, "When do you plan to go back?" I put it in the most naïve possible way, and there's only been one instance where somebody's gotten upset with me for asking that question. Usually, they get really thoughtful and they say things like, "Well, I've been here for 20 years, and I thought I would go back very soon, but I just sort of got caught up in things." And I ask if they've gone and visited their homeland: "Oh yes!" A lot of these people, especially if they come from Asia or Africa or the Middle East, they don't feel like they're Americans. They feel like they're exiled Afghans or exiled Eritreans or whatever.

VD: It's not difficult for me to understand this because I've lived in Europe now for nearly 20 years, but we made the decision to leave permanently and we have pretty fully integrated here. We don't go back, we don't visit. We're still culturally American in a number of ways, but that's partly because it's difficult to escape American culture due to the way in which it dominates entertainment.

GJ: Right.

VD: But to me it's always funny that I left so long ago and people will say to me, "Oh, well, you're still American" and then I say, "Well, why do you think that someone from El Salvador who's only been there for five years is an American?"

GJ: Right. Exactly.

VD: It makes no sense.

GJ: I have been in conversation with certain liberal academic types who within a five minute period will talk about horrible tragedies of discrimination, etcetera, the bloodshed between the Irish and the English, this horrible, horrible, long, dark history. And then within five minutes will be talking about how glorious it is that there are Pakistanis and Bangladeshis living in England.

It's like, "If two peoples as similar as the Irish and the English have this long tragic history of bloodshed, why do you think it will be any different and any better with people who are so radically different?"

VD: And that's my concern, especially in Europe, because this whole Syrian migration crisis didn't begin all that long ago, and yet you're already seeing fairly totalitarian laws in places like Hungary and stuff. They just passed a law last Friday where they can search your house without a warrant if they're looking for migrants.

GJ: Right.

VD: And this is like, what? A couple of weeks in? Can you imagine what sort of laws they're going to be passing, and what they're going to be permitting, and what the governments are going to be doing if they don't get this flow to stop fairly quickly?

GJ: Right.

VD: I'm afraid that it is going to be absolutely horrific. The problem is it's the open borders people who are completely to blame. None of this needed to happen. This is a completely unnecessary crisis that has been created.

GJ: I agree. It sort of illustrates Sam Francis's notion of anarcho-tyranny too because, on the one hand, if you're a Hungarian citizen, this is profoundly upsetting, and it's basically an across-the-board loss for you if you're a Hungarian citizen. For the Hungarian government, though, they have to have some little area of their consciousness where they realize that they benefit from this.

Nietzsche once said that "the kings of Europe never sat so securely on their thrones than since the anarchists started throwing bombs at them" and why is that? Well, because it allows them to clamp down on their populations. It allows them to have an emergency to arrogate power, to do something.

VD: The thing that's actually slightly alarming about Hungary is that this is not the extremists that are passing these laws. This is like the equivalent of the Republicans taking action.

GJ: Oh yeah.

VD: This is not Jobbik, who is to the Right of the current government, and then they've got the Arrow Cross beyond that. I think that we're basically two election cycles from the nationalists taking power, which would be a good thing. But my concern is that if the nationalists are prevented from taking power, then you're going to see the ultras eventually taking over simply because people are not going to tolerate this constant invasion, the rapes of the native populations, and the criminality and the ghettos.

When I was in Paris—it wasn't that same trip, but on another trip to Paris—it was extremely comical in a dark way, if you've got a black sense of humor. I was walking through the Jardin Nelson Mandela, which is a garden square dedicated to Nelson Mandela just outside Les Halles.

GJ: Oh, spare me. God.

VD: And there were about 60 Africans just kind of lounging around. Not causing any trouble. Just hanging out and enjoying the sun, which was fine. And there were four French gendarmes, armed with machine guns, who were standing on a platform overlooking them and keeping an eye on them all.

GJ: Right.

VD: I was just thinking that I don't think this is quite what they had in mind when they decided to honor Nelson Mandela there.

GJ: Right. It's a very, very disturbing thing. I do think this is good for nationalism in Europe, and I think that the Europeans will save themselves from this. I am less certain about the United States, because I think the United States has a very, very weak sense of identity. It's largely a propositional form of identity rather than a racial or ethnic form of identity. Those are shallow roots and we have this idea that we assimilated the Italians and the Irish, so why can't we assimilate Hispanics and Fijians and Africans? What's the difference?

VD: I'm the great-grandson of a Mexican revolutionary myself and there are Spanish-speakers in my extended family. I wouldn't say that I am of Hispanic culture. I'm more tangential to it, but the thing that people don't understand about Hispanics is that they do have functional cultures. I mean, the way that they live works, but it's very, very different than American culture. You can see it when you go south of Los Angeles now. It's not entirely Third World, but it's not First World either. They don't live like Europeans do.

GJ: Right.

VD: We were driving through Switzerland once and we saw this woman who was actually vacuuming the sidewalk.

GJ: That's great!

VD: That would never, ever happen in a Hispanic community. They just don't keep things up. They're not as uptight about that sort of thing, and that's not all bad. Where we live, it's actually similar in some ways because, you know, "Don't worry about it. You can deal with the problem tomorrow. The problem is still going to be there tomorrow. Don't worry about today. Let's just have a drink and enjoy the nice weather." It's not a horrible thing, it's not a bad thing, but you're not going to get to the Moon that way.

GJ: Right. Exactly. An Italian friend of mine years ago said that his mother or grandmother had this saying that, "Every morning the housewives of Switzerland sweep the streets and deposit the dust over Italy." So, it doesn't surprise me now that they're using vacuum cleaners. That's a new one on me. I'm going to steal that as a story.

One of the things that struck me as a point of disagreement with your book, and it's not an explicit point in your book that I was disagreeing with but sort of an assumption, is that you don't seem to think that identity politics as such is legitimate. Is that correct or was I just reading that into it?

VD: It depends what the identity politics are. I think that nationalism and tribalism are not only legitimate, I think they're virtually unstoppable forces.

GJ: Okay. That's useful. Thank you.

VD: But I think that identity politics of the sort where you decide that you're really a dragon and I decide that I'm really a little girl... that's just absurd. That's not real. It's a false form of identity politics. The thing is that the Left either denies or embraces the first form of identity politics depending upon what the identity is. Ironically, it's fine to practice Hispanic identity politics even though virtually no Hispanic people consider themselves Hispanic.

GJ: Right.

VD: My relatives are Mexican. They're not Hispanic.

GJ: Right.

VD: They don't think of themselves as Hispanic or Latino or whatever even though the SJWs recognize that identity. But the SJWs don't recognize the White Anglo-Saxon identity although it observably exists. You're not allowed to have a political identity that's based on it.

GJ: Right.

VD: You can, of course, declare yourself Otherkin and then we're all supposed to respect the idea that you're really a llama.

GJ: Right. Exactly. So much of the Left now seems to be humoring and patronizing crazy people.

VD: I think it has something to do with something that both Orwell and Dalrymple have said, which is that once you can convince someone to accept the idea that 2 + 2 = 5, you can get them to accept anything.

GJ: Right.

VD: So, they don't care what the lie is. They just want you to indicate that you are willing to submit to it, because it's the lie, it's the fact of the lie, that is the important thing. And I think that's one of the reasons why I am going to be very unpopular in certain circles, because my single guiding point is to try to ascertain the small T truth in the name of the large T Truth, and that's what I try to stand by. I don't really concern myself much with whether it makes you feel bad, or someone else feel bad, or even me feel bad. There are a lot of uncomfortable truths out there that I would like to be able to reject myself, but that way lies madness.

GJ: Right. Exactly. The main objection that I have to mainstream conservatism in the United States is that it will not embrace identity politics for White people. The battle in America today is a battle of identity politics, but they want to remain above that. The enemy is invading us from the North. They're invading us along the identity front, fighting us on the identity front, and mainstream conservatives refuse to go where the battle is. They refuse to engage on issues of identity. Instead they want to go fight on another front, right? They're not engaging the enemy and I don't think they can win that way.

VD: They can't win that way, but one of the fundamental problems that you also have is that in the same way that there's no genuine Hispanic identity, there is no White identity either. If you talk to someone, whether you do it now or you did it 30 years ago, if I went up to my friend and said, "Hey, what are you?" he wouldn't say that he was White. He would say that he was Swedish and Norwegian, and so I think that the attempt to build any sort of White identity politics suffers from the same problem that the Hispanics have.

And if you think about it, the Hispanic identity has been very unsuccessful politically compared to its numbers.

GJ: How so?

VD: Well, if you just look at the number of "Hispanic" people in California, and you look at the number of Hispanic politicians, they are woefully underrepresented. It's only very recently that the first Hispanic mayor of Los Angeles was elected despite the fact that they have theoretically had the numbers to be basically dictating everything in California for years now. But like the Anglos, as they call Whites, they do not have that Hispanic identity. They're Mexican, they're El Salvadoran, they're Guatemalan, and so forth. So the challenge is not just the fear of being called names. It's also the fact that there is no White identity per se. There are the different European nations, and there are the echoes of them in the USA.

GJ: I think yes and no. I had a meeting in California. It was a gathering of *Counter-Currents* writers and readers and donors. I think there were 38 of us in the room, and I asked how many of the people present were of some kind of unmixed European ethnic group, meaning that they weren't German-Norwegian-Spanish or whatever, that they were just Scottish or German. It turns out that only 2 people in the room were of unmixed European ethnicity, and both of them had been born outside the United States. One was born in Germany, one was born in Scotland.

VD: I understand that, but you're talking about DNA there.

You're not talking about culture. You're not talking about the way that they were raised and how they identify themselves. The sense of national identity is so much stronger in Europe than in America.

GJ: Oh, I totally agree with that.

VD: You can't even compare it. What I'm saying is that is part of the challenge I've never heard anyone talking about. It's just the fact that the White identity isn't any stronger than *la raza cósmica*, as the Hispanic intellectuals call themselves, the cosmic race.

GJ: I think that is changing, because I think that in the United States what you're getting is a kind of generic European.

VD: But you're not. That's the thing. I've written on this several times. People say we successfully integrated the Irish, we successfully integrated the Italians, and all that. We didn't really. If you look at the political history of the USA, it is very, very clear that the Irish, the Italians, and especially the Germans and Scandinavians in the Midwest— not the Germans who came first, but the Germans who came later and settled in the Midwest—they have never, ever understood the rights of Englishmen. They never had any history of it.

The whole Magna Carta, limited government, Rights of Englishmen and all that sort of thing is totally and utterly foreign to the European immigrant populations that came in the later waves. I don't think it's an accident that if you look at a lot of the crucial changes that took place, especially when you get to the 1965 Immigration and Nationality Act, I don't think it's an accident that you had the Irish grandson of immigrants and the Jewish grandson of immigrants who had a very different perspective on immigration than the Anglo-Saxons who settled the country in the first place.

That's not a hill I'm willing to go to battle on just because it's a huge subject, and it's not one that I've seen very well studied, but I do think it's a mistake to simply assume that all these people coming from Napoleonic law, Roman law traditions get the English Common Law tradition because they came from these different intellectual traditions. I don't think that they really ever truly grasped some of the concepts involved and I think that has something that factored in to how the USA was transformed over the last 60–70 years.

GJ: Yeah, I can see your point there. Again, 1965 is 50 years ago. There have been two generations since then. I meet people who have fascinating exotic German names and I'll ask them, "Wow. What an interesting German name! Where does that come from?" They don't even know it's a German name anymore, right? They're just a generic White American, middle class person. I do think that's happening more and more. I know this Greek guy and I asked him about his ancestry, where his family came from in Greece, things like that. Well, that was two generations ago. Doesn't mean anything to him.

VD: Sure, but the problem is that the fact that they're generic, and they don't know anything, and they're just generic White doesn't mean that they're going to care about the generic White thing in the way that their Lutheran Scandinavian grandparents would have cared about that identity. I think that what you're going to see is that it won't be until people begin to suffer from the aggressive identity politics of other groups that their own identity begins to really coalesce and harden.

GJ: Exactly. And I think that you might not be interested in White identity, but your enemies see you as a generic White guy.

VD: Yes, exactly. Well, not me, because I'm Indian and Mexican, but yes.

GJ: Hell, your SJW enemies still want to call you a generic White guy.

VD: That's true.

GJ: Which I think is fascinating.

VD: I love the fact that these monolingual idiots who are just white, white, white liberals, try to get on my back about being a white Republican conservative guy when I speak Italian, German, French, and some Japanese, I haven't lived in the States for most of my adult life, and I've never voted for a Republican for president.

GJ: Right.

VD: They're so focused on this template of the enemy that if you're in opposition to them they're going to cram that square peg into that round hole by any means necessary.

GJ: Exactly. They have a script and nothing's going to get in
      the way of reading their script out.

      Let's talk about the *SJWs Always Lie* book. Why do they
      always lie? What's going on there?

VD: I think that first and foremost it begins as a defense mech-
      anism. Most of the serious SJWs that you encounter are
      people who have had very difficult childhoods and have
      been dealt unfortunate hands by fate. It's not at all uncom-
      mon that if you go to an SJW-heavy site you will see that
      most of the commentators talk openly about the drugs
      that they're on. They're almost all diagnosed with some
      form of depression or anxiety or something. So, they're
      very, very fearful people, and reality is simply too much
      for them to handle, and so they retreat into a fantasy land.
      Then they attempt to make that fantasy land real in the
      same way that advertising companies do.

      You know, if you just keep telling yourself that you're really
      a girl, then eventually maybe you and the people around
      you will start to believe it. It's totally insane. It's not true,
      but they're basically trying to fake it until they make it,
      never mind that they're never, ever going to make it.

GJ: Right. When I look at people like this I just think Ni-
      etzsche was right. There are people who basically create
      ethical codes to put themselves in a flattering light. Some
      of these people seem really, really ill-favored by nature,
      right?

VD: Yes.

GJ: So, they're going to create an ethical code that not only makes them look good, but actually places them in the vanguard of humanity. So, they go about doing that. They choose their beliefs according to what makes them feel good about themselves, which is an inherently dishonest premise to begin with, and if that's the starting point, well, everything after that is basically going to be one lie after another to keep the original lie afloat.

The idea that "race" and "gender"—I'm holding my fingers in the air making scare quotes—and things like that are all social constructs, that's just a metaphysical posit, a metaphysical presupposition of this egalitarian plastic ideology that they want to have where you can basically be anything and all the differences that make people feel bad can be ironed out, can be removed somehow through social progress.

VD: Right.

GJ: It's something that I actually try to insulate myself from. I don't need to be reminded constantly about how crazy the Left is, and so reading your book and especially reading some of the quotes in there, some of these incredibly crass quotes, really was a rather upsetting experience. It's like, this is why I don't read Gawker.

But you've been in the trenches, and I realized that a lot of the people that I've gotten to know recently really are in the trenches fighting this stuff and rolling it back, and I missed out on all of that. That's one of the things that was so exciting about the book. Reading about Gamergate, which only sort of showed up on the edge of my attention, it was nothing that I really looked into, or all this stuff about the Hugo Awards and things like that which I'd never heard of, all of this stuff did not enter my world really, and so seeing how you and people associated with Gamergate actually rolled back some of this political correctness in one area of culture and then again in the sci-fi area was really inspiring.

I'm now looking at people who are in the trenches on comment boards, creating memes, and things like that. This really is the front line of the culture wars. It was very inspiring to me, and I think it would be inspiring to a lot of my readers who are equally out of touch as me, to see that this actually can be rolled back and how to do it.

So, do you have advice for people who actually want to get into the trenches and roll back PC?

VD: Well, I think the first advice is don't be afraid. One of the main reasons that people don't stand up to these people is that they're afraid. They're afraid to be called names, or they're afraid to be called racist, sexist, homophobic, etc. The thing to keep in mind is that they're just words.

GJ: Right.

VD: There are times when you're going to suffer for speaking the truth. There are times when you're going to lose opportunities or you're going to have negative experiences as a result, but the reward that comes from the self-confidence and self-respect of knowing what you said was true, and knowing that it doesn't matter if 100 other people are claiming that there are not four lights, but five, when you can see that there are four right there, is worth it.

The thing that is so important to remember is that each person who stands up and says no inspires numerous others. Maybe it's one other person, maybe it's 100 others. You don't know, and most of the time you won't even know what sort of positive impact you're having on other people. But that's why I think it's important to look to those who are already doing it, see how they're doing it, and then learn from them.

Appendix B:

The Parable of the Good Cuckservatan

A man was going down from Jerusalem to Damascus, when he was attacked by robbers. They stripped him of his clothes, beat him and went away, leaving him half dead.

A Democrat happened to be going down the same road, and when she saw the man, she passed by on the other side, telling herself that it was the Federal government's job to do something about it. She felt really bad about it, though, and she tweeted a photo of the man she'd taken along with a sad face emoji and the hashtag #justawful.

So too, a Republican, when he came to the place and saw him, passed by on the other side, figuring that this was just the sort of thing for which he paid his taxes. They were too high anyway, but he felt good that in at least this one case, they would be paying for something worthwhile. The sight of the man reminded him that he'd been intending to sell his shares in Adeptus Health, so he logged into E-Trade and made a 12 percent profit.

But a Cuckservatan, as he traveled, came where the man was; and when he saw him, he took pity on the robbers who had fallen so low as to be reduced to making a living by robbery. He went to the robbers and invited them to move into an empty house in his neighborhood, then took up a collection demanding money from his neighbors so that the robbers could bring their wives, and children, and parents, and cousins to join them and live in the nice suburban neighborhood.

When his neighbors complained that their cars were being stolen, their homes were being burgled, their lawns were being trashed, their daughters were being raped, their sons were being beaten, and their taxes were being raised without their consent, the Cuckservatan told them that they were racists, and shrieking, bigoted cowards, and they could just leave the neighborhood if they didn't like it.

Which of the three passersby would you prefer to be your neighbor? And which of them do you think will be the first against the wall when the revolution comes?

And as for what happened to the man attacked by robbers... nobody knows. Nobody cares. After all, what is the point in actually helping those in need when there is virtue to be signaled at the expense of your neighbors?

SEP 1 3 2017

CPSIA information can be obtained
at www.ICGtesting.com
Printed in the USA
LVOW03s1431160817
545245LV00012B/702/P

9 789527 065723